Immersive Learning

Immersive Learning

A Practical Guide to Virtual Reality's Superpowers in Education

Craig Frehlich

ROWMAN & LITTLEFIELD
Lanham • Boulder • New York • London

Published by Rowman & Littlefield
An imprint of The Rowman & Littlefield Publishing Group, Inc.
4501 Forbes Boulevard, Suite 200, Lanham, Maryland 20706
www.rowman.com

6 Tinworth Street, London, SE11 5AL, United Kingdom

Copyright © 2020 by Craig Frehlich

All rights reserved. No part of this book may be reproduced in any form or by any electronic or mechanical means, including information storage and retrieval systems, without written permission from the publisher, except by a reviewer who may quote passages in a review.

British Library Cataloguing in Publication Information Available

Library of Congress Cataloging-in-Publication Data
Names: Frehlich, Craig, 1970– author.
Title: Immersive learning : a practical guide to virtual reality's superpowers in education / Craig Frehlich.
Description: Lanham : Rowman & Littlefield, [2020] | Includes bibliographical references. | Summary: "VR should be used as a medium to help students bridge the gap between knowledge and concepts"— Provided by publisher.
Identifiers: LCCN 2020011075 (print) | LCCN 2020011076 (ebook) | ISBN 9781475857931 (cloth) | ISBN 9781475857948 (paperback) | ISBN 9781475857955 (epub)
Subjects: LCSH: Virtual reality in education. | Learning, Psychology of. | Education—Curricula.
Classification: LCC LB1044.87 .F75 2020 (print) | LCC LB1044.87 (ebook) | DDC 371.33/44678—dc23
LC record available at https://lccn.loc.gov/2020011075
LC ebook record available at https://lccn.loc.gov/2020011076https://lccn.loc.gov/2020011076

Contents

Preface		ix
Introduction		xiii
1	VR and Conceptual Understanding	1
2	The Importance of VR Lesson Guides	5
3	Cooperative Learning and VR	9
4	Social VR and Education	13
5	VR and Art Education	17
6	VR and Puzzle Games	21
7	VR and the STEM Curriculum	25
8	VR and Storytelling	29
9	VR for Health and Wellness	33
10	VR and Social Studies	37
Conclusion		41
Appendix A		45
VR Lesson Guides for Cooperative Learning and Communication		45
Lesson Guide: Cooperation and Working as a Team		46
Lesson Guide: Effective Decision-Making under Pressure		48
Lesson Guide: Effective Two-Way Communication		50

Appendix B	53
VR Lesson Guides for Art Education	53
Lesson Guide: VR as a Tool to Preserve Culture	54
Lesson Guide: Interrogating Scale, Space, and Place	56
Lesson Guide: Can VR Archive History?	58
Appendix C	61
VR Lesson Guides for Problem Solving and Puzzles	61
Lesson Guide: The Key to Problem Solving	62
Lesson Guide: Elastic Thinking Improves Problem-Solving	64
Lesson Guide: Form and Function in Virtual Reality	67
Appendix D	69
VR Lesson Guides for STEM Education	69
Lesson Guide: Simple Machines Make Our Lives Easier	70
Lesson Guide: Heart Physiology and Gender	72
Lesson Guide: Using VR to Connect with Nature	74
Lesson Guide: How Can We Stop Pollution?	76
Lesson Guide: Who Is the Smartest?	78
Lesson Guide: VR as a Tool for Embodiment	80
Lesson Guide: Is Diet Related to Survival?	83
Lesson Guide: Controlling the Flow of Energy	85
Lesson Guide: Adapting to the Changing Environment	88
Lesson Guide: Catapults and Levers	90
Lesson Guide: Using VR to Understand the Scale of the Universe	93
Lesson Guide: Adapting for Life on Land	95
Appendix E	97
VR Lesson Guides for Storytelling and Narrative Education	97
Lesson Guide: The Efficacy of VR Legends	98
Lesson Guide: VR as a Medium for Storytelling	100
Lesson Guide: Can VR Enhance Our Understanding of Characters in a Narrative?	102
Lesson Guide: The Interrogation of VR Storytelling	104
Lesson Guide: The Domino Effect of Storytelling	106
Lesson Guide: A Journey through Bipolar Disorder	108
Lesson Guide: Exploring Our Changing Identity	110
Appendix F	111
VR Lesson Guides for Health, Physical Education, and Wellness	111
Lesson Guide: VR as an Exercise Machine	112
Lesson Guide: Can VR Enhance Our Baseball Hitting Skills?	114
Lesson Guide: Can VR Help Refine Our Athletic Skills?	117
Lesson Guide: Can VR Help Refine Our Athletic Skills?	119
Lesson Guide: VR as a Tool for Safe Anonymous Introspection	121

Lesson Guide: Can VR Help Refine Our Athletic Skills?	123
Lesson Guide: VR as a Tool for Mindfulness and Meditation	125
Lesson Guide: Can VR Help Refine Our Athletic Skills?	127
Appendix G	129
VR Lesson Guides for Social Studies Education	129
Lesson Guide: The Future of Transportation	130
Lesson Guide: A Miner's Life	132
Lesson Guide: VR as an Empathy Machine	134
Lesson Guide: Firefighter Safety Training in VR	136
Lesson Guide: VR as a Tool for Skill Development	138
Lesson Guide: VR and Eco-tourism	140
Lesson Guide: Conflict Resolution Tactics	142
Bibliography	145
About the Author	151

Preface

> If a picture is worth a thousand words, then VR experiences are worth a million.
>
> —Anonymous

Most people want to reach their maximum potential, and the use of tools is no different. Some say power is influence. If this is true, then virtual reality (or VR) has "superpowers" because of its ability to make the unreal viscerally real, engaging, and immersive. Thanks to these powers, VR can influence and affect education in ways that no technology tool has in the past. This book will help people understand the power and true potential of virtual reality. The prime directive of this book is to provide educators with a way of thinking about how to use virtual reality in education in order to reveal its true superpowers, as well as to arm educators with several hands-on lessons on implementing VR as a tool to enhance learning outcomes. Ultimately, the book aims to have educators clearly understand VR's role in transforming education, thus reaching its maximum potential.

Having a tool to enhance learning is not new. Tools have historically helped the human species elevate its curiosity and powers of learning since the dawn of time. For example, the discovery of fire played an essential role in the evolution of the human brain, enabling people to start asking questions like why and how? Fire provided early humans opportunities to explore new places and environments and experience more of the world.[1]

In the 1990s, when the internet first connected to schools, each class was given one computer to use with students. The computer sat at the back of the room, and a few teachers, being early adopters of technology, were eager to use it in approaches to teaching and learning; however, it was mostly a research tool. Teachers would send students to look things up online instead of going to the library to access encyclopaedias or other books. The computer gave quick access to facts and knowledge. Initially, this experience was exciting for students. There was a newness and novelty about going onto the internet. Within a few months, this feeling went away, and many students lost interest in internet research. Then teachers stumbled across the work of Bernie Dodge from San Diego State University. Dodge was the godfather of the WebQuest. WebQuests were inquiry-based learning activities that used the web as a tool to gather information and connect it to more critical real-world, authentic learning outcomes. According to webquest.org, tens of thousands of teachers have embraced WebQuests as a way to make good use of the internet while engaging their students in the kinds of thinking that twenty-first-century learning requires.[2]

At its core, virtual reality is an emerging new technology tool that allows people to approach visual information in a new way, very similar to when the computer and the internet were first introduced to schools in the 1990s. This book is about how educators can approach and use this tool to ensure students are maximizing their experiences in VR. As educators get to know and understand VR, it will be essential to use it to stimulate thinking, as Bernie Dodge did for use in the early days of computers and the internet. This book will challenge the reader not to use VR as another library, but as a tool to extend students' learning.

WELCOME TO FANTASY ISLAND

One of the most popular television shows during the 1970s and 1980s was *Fantasy Island*. This American drama series, created by Gene Levitt, featured mild-mannered Mr. Roarke and his exuberant sidekick, Tattoo. People would come to the island to have their dreams or fantasies come true. Mr. Roarke was portrayed as having supernatural powers that enabled him to design experiences that were not possible in the real world. Every episode always came with a warning, "Once the fantasy is started, the guest must let it play out to its conclusion." There was always a lesson to be learned after each experience for the guest. Lessons about morality, rights and responsibilities, power and influence, and love were universal among the 152 episodes.[3]

VR is a lot like *Fantasy Island*, a portal into a new world. With its superpowers to create almost any experience possible, educators need to be deliberate about ensuring that students have made sense of these experiences. While the lessons may not be codified when participants take the headsets off, the impact of that experience needs to leave a lasting imprint. In this book, teachers will learn how to harness these superpowers to ensure that these intensely formative VR experiences shape the learning of the users in a positive direction.

This book is a journey; enjoy the ride.

NOTES

1. Mario Livio, *Why?: What Makes Us Curious* (New York: Simon & Schuster, 2017).
2. Bernie Dodge, San Diego State University, WebQuest.Org: Home, accessed January 25, 2020, http://webquest.org.
3. "Fantasy Island," Wikipedia, the Free Encyclopedia, last modified December 21, 2019, https://en.wikipedia.org/wiki/Fantasy_Island.

Introduction

> A lot of people who have not tried VR don't get it. And, once they put on a headset, the magic happens, and it is a game changer.
>
> —Ryan Schultz

WHY VIRTUAL REALITY?

Many people are fascinated and enthralled with science fiction: the popularity of Isaac Asimov novels and people lining up for hours to watch the latest Star Wars and Star Trek movies are just two good examples. The newness and advanced technology in science fiction offers a sense of awe, curiosity, and wonder about what the world might be like in the future. Although the lightsaber from Star Wars and holodeck from Star Trek are not available for use (yet), one tool or gadget is gaining massive popularity in many aspects of a technology-focused society. It is virtual reality (VR).

Most individuals have an origin story when it comes to encountering immersive virtual reality for the first time. I first became interested in immersive VR two years ago when my teenage son wanted to stop by the Microsoft Store at the local mall to test one that was on display. After signing many permission forms and waivers, he and I donned an HTC Vive, and we were immersed in a whole new world. I was impressed with the realism and quality of the experience, and played a game designed by Valve called "The Lab." There were many small experiences, but the one that made the most significant impact was "Longbow."

In Longbow, the user used a bow and arrow to target small creatures trying to attack the user's castle. As players draw back the string on the bow and arrow, they get a subtle buzzing in their VR controller that makes it feel like they are actually playing with a bow and arrow. On our drive home, we talked about how powerful this tool would be for students in the classroom. Since then, it has been my mission to learn more about how virtual reality could be beneficial for educators.

I host a podcast called *VR in Education*, and one of my first questions to people on the show is, "[w]hat got you interested in VR?" Answers to this question vary greatly. Some say they have been regular computer game users and made the jump to VR because it seemed like a natural next step. Others were inspired and fascinated by pop culture and movies like *Lawnmower Man* and *Ready Player One*. A few were invited by friends to try VR in their homes and have never looked back. Some talked about being coached by a champion in their school who was already using VR. But one common thread that weaves through everyone's origin story is the magic of VR. Here are some comments sifted from the many stories and vignettes surrounding my VR work:

- "Nothing short of mesmerizing, where do I buy one of these?" (Anonymous Grade 10 student)
- "This is way better than I expected, you feel like you are actually inside the spaceship." (Anonymous teacher)
- "In school and classes, we learn a lot from books, but in VR you can see the world." (Anonymous Grade 11 student)
- "I cannot believe this technology is here already; I thought it only existed in the movies. This is incredible." (Zain, co-host of *Everything Virtual*)

What makes VR such a worthy tool? Although this list is not exhaustive, it is clear that VR has many benefits to students and teachers in educational settings.

- Gamification of learning—Students love to play computer games. Most find the games motivating and fun because the consequence of failing is minimal. It might take several tries or attempts for a player to reach a stage or level in a game. This "level-up" mentality builds resilience and grit without the high emotional cost of being judged. A growing number of learning-type games in VR allow students to play, fail, and try again.
- Multidisciplinary—Virtual reality applications are available for many subjects and disciplines. There are applications for science, geography, history, language arts, music, art, physical education, health and wellness, and even math. Because VR is a platform where users can create and experience anything, the only limit to its connection to learning is the imagination of the developers.
- Instilling empathy—Students are often asked to "put themselves in someone else's shoes" or "see through another person's eyes." In virtual reality, this perspective building is more than a symbolic statement. Participants in the virtual world can literally see and experience what it's like to be a Syrian refugee or a homeless person living in a ghetto. As readers will learn later in this book, VR can be an empathy machine. Dr. Mannion in his research summarizes the hype and potential benefits of VR in education best: "Lessons from the pioneers

indicate that VR/AR is not just another way of conveying information; there is something distinctively powerful about the fact that the viewer is in control. This makes the experience active, and so immersive that it evokes an emotional as well as a rational response."[1]

- Creation is easy—With the rise of "design thinking" and the "maker movement" teachers are increasingly pressured to enable students to learn through creation. Virtual reality applications provide students the opportunity to design and create without physical materials and the mess that comes along with the process. They can walk around a virtual space from all angles and positions to interrogate and gain new perspectives not always possible in the real world.

- Make the impossible possible—Experience is often the best teacher. Rich multidimensional events, like travel and field trips, can transform thinking. Remember the Magic School Bus? Sweet Miss Frizzel would take her students on field trips that were beyond their wildest dreams. If they were studying blood, they could shrink down and travel inside a human artery. If they were discussing the American Civil War, they would go back in time to experience it firsthand. With virtual reality, these situations are all possible. Immersive virtual reality allows users to embody situations that might be too dangerous or even impossible in the real world. VR is not only an empathy machine, it is also an experience machine. Virtual reality can take participants to places they have never been to see and think about concepts from new perspectives.

Moreover, VR can act as an instrument for cognitive enhancement. Take juggling as an example. The barrier to entry for a beginning juggler is high. Gravity forces the juggling balls down faster than the hand, eye, and brain can learn the rhythm and pattern necessary to elevate three or more balls in the air simultaneously. However, in a VR program like Modbox, the user can scale down the force of gravity and use balls that fall slower. As the brain gets used to the technique, the user can slowly adjust the force of gravity to normal.

- A tool that sparks curiosity

Curiosity is the engine of discovery.

—Livio

It's hard to be curious about everything. Yet curiosity is a portal to deep learning. The great physicist and thinker Richard Feynman said in his last dying moments, "I don't know anything but I do know that everything is interesting if you go into it deeply enough."[2] According to Mario Livio, the necessary condition of being curious has nothing to do with being smart or good at math and art; it has to do with information processing. When information is presented in an interesting and engaging manner, individuals become naturally curious. Livio proclaims that studies have shown that when people are presented with unusual, surprising, or complex situations, like what is possible in VR, those circumstances elicit enhanced attention and curiosity.

This craving for knowledge indicative of being curious can be triggered by certain situations. Livio states that curiosity can be enhanced through novelty, rewards, or goals built into the process, and provides a challenge that is not easy or difficult. Livio added that with greater amounts of curiosity, humans increase their capacity to remember.[3] When peoples' curiosity is piqued, studies have found that people learn better and information is retained for longer.[4] VR can enhance this innate desire to learn something fully and deeply, thanks to the affordance that is provided within the tool. VR can spark increased interest and curiosity. Users can walk around a space to explore and discover. Furthermore, they can grab and manipulate objects in order to probe, question, and become more curious. Ultimately, learners learn best when attention increases. VR has the capacity to capture a user's full attention.

The Devil Is in the Details

Many people who put on a high-end VR headset feel a sense of rapture, emotion, and happiness. But these initial experiences will wear off. Just like any technology, it is only a tool or means to facilitate learning. VR headsets are "the how"; however, educators need to consider the "what and why." Process is often more important than product. In a recent podcast by Jake Miller called *Educational Duct Tape*, he differentiates between "verbs" and "nouns." Educators should focus on the "verbs," which are action words like communicating, collaborating, debating, analyzing, interrogating, and problem-solving. The "nouns" in education are the tools used to help students do these things.[5] These might involve educational technologies, like Pear Deck, Google Classroom, and a host of VR applications.

So how do teachers make the "verb" the main focus and not the "noun" in the world of VR? The emphasis in VR must be on the learning experiences. It is paramount that educators ensure that when users put on a VR headset they are focusing on deep learning.

The short answer is, have a plan. Making sense of our experience whether on vacation, a field trip, or in VR requires careful reflection and contemplation. I like to use the acronym CRISP to ensure VR experiences are rich, powerful, and engaging for students. CRISP stands for:

- C—conceptual based
- R—real world
- I—interrogative
- S—linked to standards
- P—purposeful

Further analysis of this acronym increases possible uses for educators.

C—Conceptual Based

VR experiences should emphasize conceptual thinking. Schools and learning are shifting away from content and focusing more on big ideas or concepts. Students can quickly look up facts and knowledge, but it is what they can do with this knowledge that matters. Instead of recalling the what (facts, dates, events), the focus should be more on big ideas. A conceptual learning experience will have students chewing on concepts like power, systems, change, development, and perspective. In a later chapter, concepts will be unpacked further.

R—Real World

Grounding VR experience in a real-world setting is paramount. Students often ask "why" they have to learn curriculum as a result of having no real-world connection. Establishing the context, or why in the real world will engage students and provide intrinsic motivation. People instinctively remember more when they have a framework for their learning. Linking VR applications to current events and issues is one way to provide real-world context.

I—Interrogative

VR experiences need to have students interrogate and reflect on what happened. This can be accomplished by providing a before, during, and after section to VR lesson plans. Allowing students to analyze, discuss, and debate through questions is one great way to ensure they are interrogating what happens in VR. Asking deeper-level questions that get students to think provocatively is the emphasis of the questions teachers ask students before, during, and after VR experiences; for example, questions like, "to what extent do you think VR was beneficial as a tool for providing empathy for homeless people?"

S—Linked to Standards

VR applications need to have a sense of purpose. Linking VR experiences to learning outcomes or standards helps provide a road map for students. Knowing what educators want students to achieve is paramount to the VR experience. Some essential learning outcomes do not need VR as a medium. For example, students who need to know what 2 × 2 equals may not need VR. However, students who are trying to evaluate systems and applications related to advances in technology might benefit from using a VR application to wrap their heads around this learning outcome. VR is not always the best tool for the job. Knowing the learning objectives or outcomes can help teachers determine whether VR would be beneficial.

P—Planned

VR experiences need to focus on a plan. Giving students a sense of order and structure to their learning will ensure that learning is maximized. Careful consideration is taken regarding what the user considers before, during, and after the VR experience to ensure participants are maximizing their learning and unlocking new perspectives. In the early days of VR applications in education, often students and teachers put on headsets without a clear understanding of the goal or plan. Providing a robust experience means giving students a sense of order in the form of a VR lesson plan or content guide. A structured blueprint or map will provide essential direction to guide the learner so they do not get lost. VR lesson plans can awaken the mind and make the learning conscious only with a clear vision of where the journey is going. VR lesson plans will be expanded on in Chapter 2 of this book.

I would like to end this chapter with a quick story and analogy. My family once hiked through the rainforest in Malaysia. We stumbled across an endangered monkey who was caught in a trap on a nearby tree. Our hiking guide explained how this happened. The monkeys are often found and tagged by the government by placing food inside a vase that has a narrow neck at the top and a wide bottom. So, the monkey will approach the vase hanging in the trees, crimp its hand to fit down the narrow neck, grab the food at the bottom, which creates a massive fist, and will not be able to remove its hand from the vase because its grip is too big. Reluctant to let go of the food in its fist, the monkey is trapped in the tree until the government officials arrive to tag the monkey and set it free again.

In education, teachers do not want students to be caught with their hand in a vase; therefore lacking any skills necessary to adapt and change. If teachers are careful to provide a CRISP learning experience in VR, they will pave the way for students to be thinkers, and not memorizers, who have the skills to cope in an ever-changing world. "Don't just think of VR as a place where you can look at a molecule in 3D, or perhaps handle one, VR is the place where you become a molecule, where you learn to think like a molecule."[6] As the reader will see in this book, rekindling curiosity and a love for learning in schools is possible with the right approach. VR is one of the emerging new tools to help learners on this journey. The premise of this book is that VR can be a powerful portal to embrace approaches to learning and curriculum that have often been difficult to address and teach in the classroom. Consider this: teaching kids to memorize is easy, but teaching kids to think deeply about concepts and ideas is messy, but fruitful.

NOTES

1. James Mannion, "Growth Headset: Exploring the Use of Virtual Reality and Augmented Reality in Schools," *Rethinking Education*, 2018.
2. Mario Livio, *Why?: What Makes Us Curious* (New York: Simon & Schuster, 2017).
3. Livio, *Why?*.
4. Matthias J. Gruber and Charan Ranganath, "How Curiosity Enhances Hippocampus-Dependent Memory: The Prediction, Appraisal, Curiosity, and Exploration (PACE) Framework," *Trends in Cognitive Sciences* 23, no. 12 (2019).
5. Jake Miller, "Marcia Kish, Blended Learning, Seesaw, Student Ownership, Learning Environments, Classroom Balance, Adjacent Possible, Focusing on Verbs More Than Nouns," last modified January 22, 2020, https://www.podbean.com/media/share/dir-4f6w8-6d34c88?utm_campaign=w_share_ep&utm_medium=dlink&utm_source=w_share.
6. Jaron Lanier, *Dawn of the New Everything: Encounters with Reality and Virtual Reality* (New York: Henry Holt and Company, 2017).

1
VR and Conceptual Understanding

> VR is amazing at turning complexity into lucidity.
>
> —Jaron Lanier

When people look up into the night sky and see the stars shine and twinkle, they are struck with awe and wonder. Why does this experience make them contemplate their place in the universe, and why does it trigger such a robust emotional response and connection?

Big ideas like this one, often triggered through experiences, help shape our thinking; for example, when we remember our school days. Many of us have sat in a classroom filled with desks lined up in rows. The teacher might have explained where the state capitals were on a map. Students would diligently take notes on this information in the hope that it would stay safely locked in their brains forever. The lesson would finish with a worksheet that asked students to "spit" back learned information. This static model of teaching and learning was how many of us experienced formal education.

WHAT IS CONCEPTUAL LEARNING?

> Nothing can be loved or hated unless it is truly understood.
>
> —Leonardo Da Vinci

The education of children is slowly shifting in the twenty-first century to a process in which learning is cradled in a more conceptual model. Concepts are enduring "big ideas" that help organize and structure facts and knowledge into more accessible, easy-to-understand "bins." Some examples of concepts worthy of learning and understanding include power, identity, systems, change, conflict, sustainability, rights, and responsibilities, whereas examples of facts and knowledge might be how many moons Mars has, who the Cuban dictator was, and parts of the heart. Mindlessly memorizing facts should not be the goal of education.

Making sense of facts through concepts enables students to develop more significant meaning and connection to the learning. There is a greater appetite for learning about whether humans are alone in the universe, a conceptual idea, than how many stars make up our universe, a factual idea. Every topic should be an ongoing journey of discovery, evolution of thought, and development of meaning. "The art and science of teaching go beyond the presentation and extraction of information. Artful teachers engage students emotionally, creatively, and intellectually to instill deep and passionate curiosity in learning."[1]

When concepts are an essential part of the curriculum, students have a heightened sense of wonder and inquiry. Educators want students to think provocatively and look closely at their learning to interrogate it and discover new meanings and relationships instead of focusing on isolated bits of information. That is not to say that facts are not important. It is hard to be curious about something one already knows, and, conversely, it is difficult to be curious about something one knows nothing about. The reason babies, infants, and toddlers are so curious is that they know just the right amount of information to wonder about the world and make bigger conceptual connections.

WHY VR FOR CONCEPTUAL LEARNING?

> If you turn complicated information into a virtual place, a palace you can roam, or a city you can explore, your brain remembers better and notices more.
>
> —Jaron Lanier

Virtual reality has a significant role to play in this conceptual model of learning. Virtual reality has been described as a powerful immersive communication tool with incredible promise in the field of education. One promise of VR is its ability to evoke emotional experiences. Due to the realism and embodiment created by VR applications, participants feel a sense of "presence."

Presence can cause the user to suspend disbelief and believe they are physically in the virtual environment, reacting to stimuli as if they were in the real world. Since VR is an experience machine, it can be used to help bridge the gap between book knowledge and concepts. Connecting facts to essential concepts is a skillful art that requires teachers to provide compelling experiences to help students inquire, think, and discover. "Students need to organize and use knowledge conceptually if we expect them to apply it beyond the classroom."[2] Presenting students with real-life experiences that connect them to relevant content and concepts helps cement their understanding. In a study done by Dr. James Mannion, who surveyed teachers regarding their perceived use of VR in their teaching, one teacher said, "I teach classics, so getting students to empathize with the remote past is difficult. When using VR/AR, you can be placed in the moment, and it helps students to understand the ancient world more. Even watching 360 YouTube videos gives them a good sense, so I feel VR/AR would give them an even greater feeling and understanding."[3]

Most students' fondest memories in school are field trips, because they make the learning purposeful and interactive. For example, a physics field trip to an amusement park where they encounter various rides, collect data, and interrogate the form and function of these machines can provide a very powerful learning experience.

EXAMPLES OF WELL-DESIGNED CONCEPTUAL VR EXPERIENCES

Many well-designed VR applications can be magical modern-day field trips with the right affordances. Here are two examples of VR applications that are firmly anchored in conceptual thinking and twenty-first-century curriculum:

- *Becoming Homeless*—Stanford VR's *Becoming Homeless* invites students to understand and empathize with the rights and responsibilities surrounding homelessness. This engaging and interactive narrative puts the participant in the shoes of a homeless person. The user learns firsthand what it is like to end up on the street. The user gets to experience selling their possessions to ward off eviction, sleeping in their car only to be approached by the police, and living on a bus where a man tries to steal their backpack. The ultimate goal is for participants to meditate on who is at fault for homelessness around the world.
- *Fantastic Contraption*—This highly appealing VR application focuses on how form is related to function. Participants can adapt, change, and redesign structures. Students learn that failure is part of the process, a vital engineering skill. Agile thinking is emphasized in this application. Students learn, try, fail, and rethink their process. In this VR application, students develop a growth mindset as they adapt their devices to meet the specific requirements of each game level.

Students must be asked to develop conceptual understandings that lead to a fuller picture of learning outcomes. In the twenty-first century, students should not be exposed to "just the facts." Teachers need to craft a variety of different lessons and learning experiences.

> "In the past, memorizing the tidy set of known facts, rules, figures and dates of any school subject was a necessary part of learning. Today, attempting to memorize the overflowing storerooms of facts and knowledge in any field is clearly impossible. But

an immense number of facts can be remembered or accessed as needed with a quick Internet search. Yet, knowing a field's core ideas, understanding its fundamental principles, and applying this knowledge to solve new problems and answer new questions are evergreen learning tasks that will never become outdated. These learning skills need to move to the heart of what our schools teach."[4]

Learning presented in a manner that allows students to question, notice, hypothesize, observe, and develop new meanings and connections tends to make them more committed to the learning activity.

The next chapter will cover how one might use lesson guides that target "big ideas." These lesson guides will act as an essential road map to help students navigate toward conceptual learning targets. Additionally, in the second part of this book, a variety of different lessons are provided that give a turnkey solution to implementing VR in education.

NOTES

1. H. L. Erickson, *Concept-Based Curriculum and Instruction for the Thinking Classroom* (Thousand Oaks, CA: Corwin Press, 2007).

2. Erickson, *Concept-Based Curriculum*.

3. James Mannion, "Growth Headset: Exploring the Use of Virtual Reality and Augmented Reality in Schools," https://iscdigital.co.uk/wp-content/uploads/2018/11/Growth-headset-final-reportV2.pdf (The Independent Schools Council (ISC) Digital Strategy Group, 2018).

4. Bernie Trilling and Charles Fadel, *21st Century Skills: Learning for Life in Our Times* (Hoboken, NJ: John Wiley & Sons, 2012).

2

The Importance of VR Lesson Guides

> An important consideration is that games (and applications) are not standalone experiences. For a game (application) to be effective, it can't just be simply dropped into a classroom, but it needs to be carefully integrated with regard to the curriculum, logistical requirements, and student needs. The context and community around it, and inside it, matters. It also requires an educator, parent, mentor, or another resource who can help support and guide the players and shape the learning experience with them.[1]
>
> —Karen Schrier

The students in classrooms today are unlike anything experienced in previous decades. Most have grown up with devices, and these students may be called digital natives. Growing up surrounded by technologies like the internet, iPads, and iPhones has created a unique persona that should be taken into account when designing learning experiences. These students approach the world differently.

According to Trilling and Fadel, digital native students want experiences that can be customized and personalized, can be scrutinized by having the ability to see behind and scenes, have an element of play and entertainment, have quick access to information with very little waiting time, and have built-in collaboration in order to form and craft relationships.[2] These characteristics require careful consideration for teachers who aspire to design lessons and learning experiences that capture the attention and interest of digital natives. Such demands require new powers of design to ensure learning is personalized, interrogative, entertaining, efficient, and collaborative.

Instructional design is the systematic planning of a lesson to ensure student learning is maximized. Master teachers meticulously orchestrate instruction so that learning comes to life. The roadmap to effective teaching and, therefore, quality learning is the lesson plan or guide. While there are myriad details that might be included in lesson guides, Singapore Management University's Centre of Excellence in Teaching suggests including three common elements: learning objectives, learning outcomes, and assessment to check for student understanding.[3] Effective teachers will consider what the student is doing prior to, during, and after the educational activity has been delivered. VR instruction is no different than regular face-to-face instruction. It is hard to reach your destination if you do not know where you are going.

In an article in *Edtech* magazine titled "Education Among the Top Industries for AR/VR investments," Melissa Delaney talks about the potential of VR in education and how VR/AR can transform the way people learn.[4] This well-written editorial draws on the expertise of Jaime Donally, author of the book *Learning Transported: Augmented, Virtual and Mixed Reality for All Classrooms*. Donally cautions educators to have a clear purpose and goal for introducing VR/AR in the classroom, "defining goals and expectations for how mixed reality integration will benefit classroom instruction. That way, students don't just go on aimless hikes through the rain forests of the Democratic Republic of Congo. Instead, they can walk in the shoes of a wildlife biologist in search of gorillas."[5]

Donally is correct. Teachers cannot assume that putting on a headset and entering a VR application will guarantee deep learning. Donally's caution can be taken a step further. Having a clear conceptual and contextual understanding regarding what educators want students to learn and experience is essential.

If lesson plans or guides are akin to "road maps" helping shepherd students on their learning journeys, then VR lesson guides might be "treasure maps." Treasure maps offer a sense of mystery and discovery. They are fun and invite the participant on a curious adventure. The path one takes is not defined by one direction; instead the map reader is taken through many twists and turns in hopes of making the abstract more concrete. Treasure hunters solve problems to reveal important clues and make connections through experience. They stretch their analytic thinking and reliance skills.

Virtual reality experiences can be awe-inspiring and magical. To ensure emotional and intellectual cognitive development in this new immersive medium, stakeholders would benefit from having a sense of direction provided by detailed VR lesson guides. VR lesson guides offer a map or framework for introspection and give participants a provocative reason to enter a VR application. These guides aim to enhance the relationship with the VR application to expand a user's world view through contextual/conceptual thinking and self-reflection. Careful consideration is taken regarding what the user considers before, during, and after the VR experience to ensure participants are maximizing their learning and unlocking new perspectives. "Education today values and promotes many brain-based strategies such as the use of essential questions, constructivism, and inquiry, yet we too often continue to publish curriculum documents and textbooks that list the same old objectives to cover."[6]

In the Netflix series *Abstract*, Ruth Carter, a famous costume designer, describes the prominent role that designers play in theater, television, and film. Costume designers ruminate over details to portray the right ethos for a character. The script is just the beginning for costume designers. They need to know how concepts like the scene, setting, and the cultural context all fit in to transform the character through costume. The color, texture, and lighting of the material that makes up the costumes are essential to help tell the story or narrative. The actor and the character need to meld with the help of good costume design. Costume design is tasked with this significant responsibility of supporting a story. It breathes life into the narrative.[7]

Like good costume designers, content designers for VR experiences play a similar role. Instead of fusing the actor with the character in a movie, VR content creators are charged with bringing or melding the realness of the virtual reality content with the real world. Educators need to work hard to ensure users have a deeply compelling experience when they put on a headset by engaging the participant in reflection before, during, and after the experience. Instead of color, texture, materials, and fabric, teachers are working with concepts, big ideas, questions, learning outcomes, and extension activities. While costume designers are concerned with problems such as whether a mesh pattern captures the tension between whites and blacks in Harlem in the early '70s, VR content designers might ask things like, does the user have a clear idea of the overall purpose of the VR engagement? What essential vocabulary and concepts do they need to be aware of before they enter the VR application? How can their learning be extended once they take off the headset to continue to evoke emotional responses?

There is no denying that theater, television, and film would be underwhelming without amazing costumes. It is the hard work of the costume designer working tirelessly behind the scenes that helps bring stories and characters to life. At the same time, magical VR experiences usually do not happen without a lot of behind-the-scenes hard work. Educators need to develop VR lesson guides to ensure each experience is impressive. Setting a user into a VR experience without the proper framework and thought guidance might be akin to throwing an actor on the stage of a Shakespeare play in Lululemon clothes. It is essential to make sure users have the right costume before they enter any VR application.

This chapter offered a clearer picture of the importance of guiding students as they embark on using VR as a powerful tool for learning. Ultimately, it is just a tool. Mark Twain once said, "[w]e should be careful to get out of a learning experience only the wisdom that is in it." With the right context, this tool can provide high leverage in the learning journey. In a blog John Spencer, coauthor of the design thinking book *Launch*, talked about the analogy of cooks and chefs. Cooks usually follow a recipe to make the same meal every time, but chefs experiment with ingredients and sometimes create new and different dishes.[8] In education, teachers want the students to be chefs who experiment with ideas through influential conceptual blueprints that invite them to think, provoke, and reflect. VR can do this with the right lesson guide. In the appendix part of this book, over 40 different lesson guides are provided that can be used to guide and enhance VR experiences for students.

NOTES

1. Karen Schrier, *Learning, Education & Games, Volume 3: 100 Games to Use in the Classroom & Beyond* (Morrisville, NC: Lulu.com, n.d).
2. Bernie Trilling and Charles Fadel, *21st Century Skills: Learning for Life in Our Times* (Hoboken, NJ: John Wiley & Sons, 2012).
3. "Lesson Planning," Centre for Teaching Excellence, n.d., https://cte.smu.edu.sg/approach-teaching/integrated-design/lesson-planning.
4. Melissa Delaney, "Survey: Education Among Top Industries for AR/VR Investments," Technology Solutions That Drive Education, last modified August 8, 2019, https://edtechmagazine.com/k12/article/2019/08/survey-education-among-top-industries-arvr-investments.
5. Delaney, "Survey: Education Among Top Industries for AR/VR."
6. H. L. Erickson, *Concept-Based Curriculum and Instruction for the Thinking Classroom* (Thousand Oaks, CA: Corwin Press, 2007).
7. *Abstract (Season 2)—Ruth Carter: Costume Designer*, directed by Netflix (Netflix, 2019).
8. John Spencer, "What Two Cooking Shows Taught Me about Design Thinking," last modified March 29, 2019, http://www.spencerauthor.com/what-two-cooking-shows-taught-me-about/.

3

Cooperative Learning and VR

> Unity is strength ... when there is teamwork and collaboration, wonderful things can be achieved.
>
> —Mattie Stepanek

Schools are starting to realize that they cannot just teach content related to subject disciplines for students to be successful beyond school. If students are to be prepared for jobs in the future that are constantly changing, then educators need to pay heed to skills related to dealing with people. The "soft skills" curriculum is becoming an essential part of what teachers need to address in their classrooms. Some examples of these skills might include social skills, empathy, confidence, leadership, collaboration, patience, and critical thinking.[1] These skills are sometimes called approaches to learning.

All teachers are responsible for explicitly teaching these skills to ensure students can succeed in an ever-changing world. Google, one of the most successful companies in the world, in 2008 published a document titled *Project Oxygen*, which outlined ten key behaviors of successful managers. On this list, communicating effectively and cooperation show up multiple times.[2] Learning how to work well in groups or take on responsibility and leadership are two examples of these critical life skills. While it is easy to pass off these skills as extraneous and not necessary, the reality is that skills like these are paramount in an ever-changing world and essential for our students to adapt and succeed.

Many adults remember playing a game called "Kick the Can" with other children. This multiplayer activity involves one person (or group of people) being "it," who has to guard the can, which might be sitting in an open field or yard. Everyone else in the game runs off to hide. After a short countdown, the person who is "it" must find and tag all participants before one of them kicks over the can. As the "it" person tags players, they must sit in a holding zone or "jail." If the can is knocked over before all the participants are "jailed," everyone captured is free to roam and continue playing.

One may not have been aware of it at the time of playing the game, but "Kick the Can" taught several life skills that define key personality traits as an adult. Trust, strategy, cooperation, leadership, and effective communication were just a few of the concepts embodied as a result of playing this cooperative learning game.

By definition, cooperative (or collaborative) learning involves small groups of people (or teams) working together to accomplish a common shared goal.

WHY VR FOR COOPERATIVE LEARNING?

VR is often seen as a solitary experience because the user dons an HMD (head-mounted display) and leaves the real world behind them. Yet there is a growing number of VR applications that rely on single VR participants to work with a group of people inside or outside the HMD forming a team. "Asymmetrical gaming is a multiplayer mode in which the different players have different roles and capabilities, unlike most multiplayer games, where all the players are generally doing the same thing and playing the game the same way."[3] VR applications that have asymmetrical features require users to work cooperatively to achieve a shared outcome. More importantly, these asymmetrical games that have one user inside the headset and the other participants playing along outside the HMD are growing in popularity.

RECOMMENDED VR COOPERATIVE LEARNING APPLICATIONS

Here are three popular cooperative asymmetrical learning VR applications for education:

- *Acron*—This is a modern-day version of Capture the Flag. In this multiplayer experience, one player in VR takes on the role of a large, ancient tree that is the protector of the acorns. Meanwhile, two to eight players outside VR can then grab their phone devices to become competing squirrels that need to come up with a strategy to steal the acorns. Cooperation among the team of squirrels is essential for success.[4]
- *Black Hat Cooperative*—This cooperative game involves two or more people. One player is in VR, sneaking past enemies and collecting treasure. Other players are on the computer and keyboard with access to a full view of the map and hacking superpowers. This game requires quick thinking, trust, effective two-way communication, and unflappable decision-making techniques.[5]
- *Keep Talking and Nobody Explodes*—This amazing team-building and communication game has one student in the HMD who sees a bomb in a room, and

the rest of the team outside the VR headset has a bomb-defusing manual. The team members must provide clear and concise information to the person in the HMD to enable her to cut wires and to defuse the bomb.[6]

IMPLICATIONS FOR EDUCATORS

There are several factors to consider before exposing students to this type of learning—merely grouping students into cooperative teams does not guarantee a positive experience.[7] Firstly, students in a group need to feel they have positive interdependence. That is to say, they need to feel "in it together." Members of the group need to know that their contributions will help move the team forward toward the goal.

Secondly, individuals within the group all need to feel engaged. Individuals need to be given agency to interact with the application and others during the experience. Heightened interaction may be facilitated through the equal distribution of resources within the experience. Thirdly, students should be coached on various types of strategies that can be employed when engaging in the cooperative learning experience.

Finally, students should be taught interpersonal skills related to how to work and communicate in a collaborative team. This may involve having explicit norms within the team, like turn-taking, decision-making, and establishing trust. With these factors in mind, students will have a more successful cooperative and collaborative learning engagement.

COOPERATIVE IS "KEY" AT ANY AGE

I was once in an airport, heading with my family on a vacation, and struck up a conversation with a pilot standing in line at Starbucks. "Do airplanes differ in controls on the right side versus the left side in the cockpit?" I asked. His response was interesting. Most airplane cockpits have similar controls on both sides. Pilots and copilots have equal and often redundant instrumentation to fly the plane. There is redundancy built into the system. "Does this often lead to conflict regarding who does what?" I asked. For his airline, the pilot and copilot work cooperatively as a team to decide who is responsible for which tasks from takeoff to landing.

They even take specific training to ensure that, although there is a hierarchical imbalance between the pilot and copilot, the strong communication between the two flight officers overcomes this power structure. He even mentioned that social norms and cultural bias toward power imbalances within a cockpit have led to crashes in the past. An overly authoritarian captain can severely exacerbate this tendency and even paralyze the copilot to the point that they become a mere bystander. This occurred during the crash of Korean Air Cargo Flight 8509. The captain, a domineering former military pilot, made a catastrophic error. The first officer noticed but did nothing, out of a fear of reprisal. The aircraft hit the ground less than sixty seconds after takeoff, killing everyone on board.[8] The pilot indicated that his company regularly trains pilots about how to cooperate as a team.

The benefits of using cooperative VR applications for learning in educational institutions are enormous. Since many schools have limited budgets, they may have only a few headsets for one large classroom. Using asymmetrical cooperative VR applications will increase the number of students that can participate in the learning experience. Additionally, there is a greater focus in schools on enhancing students' "soft skills." In a world that is ever-changing, one thing is for sure: teaching students how to work more effectively to strategize in a group or team is always important and relevant.

For examples of lesson guides related to cooperative learning in VR, please see **Appendix A** at the end of this book.

NOTES

1. H. L. Erickson, *Concept-Based Curriculum and Instruction for the Thinking Classroom* (Thousand Oaks, CA: Corwin Press, 2007).
2. "Project Oxygen—Google Spent 10 Years Researching What Makes the Perfect Manager," Eden Tech Labs, last modified December 10, 2019, https://www.edentechlabs.io/post/project-oxygen-google-spent-10-years-researching-what-makes-the-perfect-manager.
3. "Asymmetric Multiplayer," TV Tropes, n.d., https://tvtropes.org/pmwiki/pmwiki.php/Main/AsymmetricMultiplayer.
4. "Acron: Attack of the Squirrels!" SpringboardVR, accessed January 26, 2020, https://springboardvr.com/marketplace/acronattackofthesquirrels.
5. "Black Hat Cooperative," SpringboardVR, accessed January 26, 2020, https://springboardvr.com/marketplace/blackhatcooperative.
6. "Keep Talking and Nobody Explodes," last modified November 9, 2018, https://keeptalkinggame.com/.
7. David M. Johnson and Roger T. Johnson, "What is Cooperative Learning?—Cooperative Learning Institute," Cooperative Learning Institute, n.d., http://www.co-operation.org/what-is-cooperative-learning.
8. Eve Fabre, "Are There Two Pilots in the Cockpit?" The Conversation, last modified April 11, 2018, http://theconversation.com/are-there-two-pilots-in-the-cockpit-94630.

4
Social VR and Education

> A wide variety of online communication tools and environments that support social, collaborative, and community approaches to learning are now available. Since the Internet is global, students can now be global learners, connecting and learning with others around the planet.[1]
>
> —Bernie Trilling and Charles Fadel

The Amanda Todd story is a harsh reminder of the complex world of online social platforms and how difficult they can be to navigate. Amanda Todd was a teenager from Port Coquitlam, British Columbia, who committed suicide due to her struggles with bullying and cyberbullying.[2] Her story evoked considerable attention to bullying, especially cyberbullying, which was considered relatively new at the time. In this example, bullying had surpassed name-calling.

Online platforms like *Facebook*, *Instagram*, and *YouTube* were front and center for the potential to cause horrific social and emotional harm to vulnerable people. It spread awareness on how to be safe and avoid predators online, and it sparked a conversation among families within Canada and all over the world about cyberbullying and online safety. Now digital citizenship, how one acts and behaves online, is an integral part of most schools' curriculum around the world. The Amanda Todd story has raised the importance of teaching students how to navigate the online world. Furthermore, schools are more cautious than ever before about protecting and safeguarding children from the feeding frenzy that might occur in online platforms.

WHAT IS SOCIAL VR?

In my recent podcast interview with Ryan Schultz, an avid blogger about social VR, he describes social VR as a place where one can gather with other people in

VR.[3] People are often embodied or represented in social VR by an avatar, which is a personal representation of oneself in VR. The user has a wide range of customizable choices regarding what their avatar looks like, and users don't have to look like their true selves in the real world. For example, in some social VR platforms, one can purchase a female body that looks like a Japanese geisha girl, allowing the user to role-play this particular character or persona. In other social VR applications, users can play dodgeball or paint together. These social gatherings give participants a sense of community.

THE BENEFITS OF SOCIAL VR

The purpose of most social VR platforms is usually open-ended, whereby one can socialize, connect, chat, role-play, and interact. Social VR lets participants be anybody and anything. It gives them a chance to be in someone else's skin to see what that feels like. There is excellent potential for social VR. People can have meetings and attend conferences without the headache or environmental impact of flying all over the world. Thanks to the affordances of VR, one is able to interact with people in an immersive experience. Nuances such as tone of voice, hand gestures, and body language give the participants a sense that they are actually with people.

Additionally, by adopting the persona of another avatar, the user might build empathy and understanding for that particular person. For example, men might become more empathetic toward women when they are asked to adopt or inhabit a female avatar for a while in social VR. With such experiences, users might alter their opinion or perspective about a particular gender, race, ethnicity, religion, or culture. Some companies are already rolling out diversity or inclusion training through the use of VR applications. For example, Equal Reality is a virtual reality program that allows users to see from another point of view.[4] It uses VR experiences highlighting various forms of bias, which are then triggered for conservations and reflections.

Social VR may also help users belong. Identifying with a community is a basic human need, and social VR may help people combat loneliness. Some social VR platforms help users find their "tribe" by grouping participants into rooms that have similar hobbies, interests, and age ranges.

Here is a list of some popular social VR sites:

- *VRChat*—*VRChat* is a free-to-play multiplayer online virtual reality social platform created by Graham Gaylor and Jesse Joudrey. It allows players to interact with others as 3D character models. Players can socialize and create different worlds together.[5]
- *Rec Room*—*Rec Room* is a place to hang out with friends from all around the world. Users can play multiplayer games like paintball or just chill in the park. Avatars can discover thousands of player-created rooms, with new ones added daily.[6]

- *AltspaceVR*—*AltspaceVR* is a virtual space to attend live shows, meetups, cool classes, and more with friendly people from around the world.[7]
- *Engage VR*—*Engage VR* is a closed and controlled social environment that creates immersive classes and hangouts. Great for educational institutions that use social VR to craft positive learning experiences.[8]

IMPLICATIONS FOR EDUCATORS

With great potential, there can also be hesitation and worry. Many educators, parents, and other people who work in the field of pastoral care are reticent about social VR. Will these new 3D platforms, which have even more significant potential to cause emotional hardship due to their high level of immersion, repeat the follies of 2D sites like *Facebook*, *Twitter*, *Instagram*, and *YouTube*? Due to the anonymity of users, it is hard to control or police the behaviors of others. In the interview with Ryan Schultz, he indicated that most social VR applications have had to implement tools to mute or block inappropriate behaviors by other avatars. However, despite these efforts there is still potential for harm within social VR platforms, especially ones that do not offer private rooms for participants.

I have personally tried the VR application *Rec Room*. I entered the open-ended platform, customized my avatar, and walked around the environment. I joined a room where people were shooting a basketball, and I attempted a few shots. A handful of avatars interacted with me by inviting me to give them a high-five or a harmless wave. My experience was entirely positive. In my 35 minutes playing *Rec Room* VR, I never encountered a single bully, troll, or negative experience, unless maybe one counts the fact that I could not make a single basketball shot! What struck me most was the feelings I experienced while meeting people in VR for the first time. Even though the avatars had origami-shaped cartoon heads, I still had this warm, visceral feeling that there were real persons in there. The sense was far more pronounced than what I experienced when I entered online internet chat rooms.

In regards to advice for educators, there is much to be learned about social platforms over the coming years, which will better prepare people to tread carefully when it comes to social VR in educational settings. As more HMDs (head mount displays) enter the educational marketplace, it will be essential to learn more about what each social VR platform offers in regards to controls and settings. Because schools act as de facto parents for students while in school, educators need to make sure children are protected from unnecessary emotional harm. Allowing students to enter open social platforms like *AltspaceVR*, *Rec Room*, and *VRChat* would be risky, whereas a system that enables teachers to control the social group would be safer. The best approach is to investigate and research highly controlled VR platforms like *Engage*, whereby the rooms, participants, and environments are safeguarded like a well-planned field trip.

There is no denying that social VR is becoming extremely popular in today's society. *Rec Room* reported at the end of 2019 that they have roughly 200 million users and over 1.6 million rooms.[9] Facebook, in November 2019, announced a new social VR platform called *Facebook Horizons*. Their goal or aim is to bring social VR to the masses. It will be necessary for schools and educators to have a strong understanding of how these new immersive social spaces operate. Thankfully, many schools around the world have already implemented digital citizenship programs that teach students ethics and values on how to behave online. Moreover, Common Sense Media has coauthored a report in partnership with Stanford University's Virtual Human Interaction Lab, which provides advice to educators, parents, and children regarding the use of virtual reality. This comprehensive guide, called *Virtual Reality 101*, explores the positive and negative implications of using VR.[10]

Recommending open-ended social VR platforms and providing sample lesson plans would be akin to telling a parent how to raise their child. Each school needs to approach this matter with caution and careful consideration. Educators should be in no rush to expose students to any unnecessary risks that could be lurking in some social VR settings.

NOTES

1. Bernie Trilling and Charles Fadel, *21st Century Skills: Learning for Life in Our Times* (Hoboken, NJ: John Wiley & Sons, 2012).

2. "The Story of Amanda Todd and the Horrific Effects of Cyberbullying," UBC Blogs, last modified November 7, 2018, https://blogs.ubc.ca/course0512e7b9763eca9657ab083805266162ded14194/2018/11/07/the-story-of-amanda-todd-and-the-horrific-effects-of-cyberbullying/.

3. Ryan Shultz, Podcast Interview, https://cfrehlich.podbean.com/e/episode-23-social-vr-and-education-with-ryan-schultz/December 13, 2019.

4. "Equal Reality: Soft Skills, Diversity and Inclusion VR Training," Equal Reality, last modified August 29, 2018, https://equalreality.com/index.

5. VRChat Inc., VRChat, accessed January 25, 2020, https://www.vrchat.com/.

6. "Rec Room on Steam," Welcome to Steam, accessed January 25, 2020, https://store.steampowered.com/app/471710/Rec_Room/.

7. AltspaceVR, AltspaceVR Inc, last modified December 29, 2014, https://altvr.com/.

8. ENGAGE Virtual Reality Education & Corporate Training. VR Education Holdings PLC, last modified August 18, 2015, https://engagevr.io/.

9. Kent Bye, "#883 'Rec Room:' Social VR World Building Platform on PC, Console, Mobile, & VR," Voices of VR Podcast, last modified June 8, 2016, https://voicesofvr.com/883-rec-room-social-vr-world-building-platform-on-pc-console-mobile-vr/.

10. "Virtual Reality 101: What You Need to Know About Kids and VR," Common Sense Media: Age-Based Media Reviews for Families, n.d., https://www.commonsensemedia.org/research/virtual-reality-101.

5
VR and Art Education

> Logic will get you from A to B. Imagination will take you everywhere.
>
> —Albert Einstein

According to the International Baccalaureate Art Guide, art is about human expression and communication. Learning through the arts invites students to investigate shape and form on a journey to discover various types of identity.[1] A strong art curriculum fosters students' curiosity about their creations as well as the designs of others. Students need to build confidence, courage, and resilience through active learning. Thinking creatively is also an important goal of the art process. Creative thinkers trust their intuition, question, contemplate independently, challenge assumptions, visualize alternatives, and experiment with ideas.

WHY DRAW IN VIRTUAL REALITY?

Designing art has always been a creative process. Students can use their imagination to craft 2D objects by hand on paper or by computer onto 2D space. In the 1960s computer-aided design, or CAD, was developed to aid artists and designers in creating more advanced models that were 3D on a two-dimensional computer screen. Drawing using CAD can be a steep learning curve for many beginners because of the difficulty associated with visualizing 3D objects in a space that is only two-dimensional. More recently, virtual reality has entered the drawing scene and has taken creative process to a new level. Virtual reality drawing applications have immense advantages compared to drawing 3D objects in CAD programs on flat two-dimensional computer screens because the user can move around their creations and visibly see the purpose in a 3D space. The visualization and interrogation of a user's piece of artwork are much more comfortable.

There is something visceral about creating art in VR. As the user's mind and body work as one in a three-dimensional space, they get emotionally drawn to their creation. As the user walks around their design, they can interrogate it from several angles. Furthermore, the artist can move in close to the design and scale it up to a larger size to create brush strokes and details not possible in a 2D space. In VR, mistakes are never permanent. With the touch of a button, the user can erase their design and start again. The process of iteration is smooth and seamless.

The student can move through the creative process free of distraction and, therefore, more open to inquiry, discovery, and experimentation. Sometimes the cost of establishing a robust art studio can be prohibitive for some schools. In VR, users have access to a variety of different resources. Most VR applications for art have a multitude of mediums, styles, and types of instruments. "When I put on the VR headset, I feel like I am in a whole new world, a world where my imagination can run wild free from the judgements and criticism of the real world."[2]

RECOMMENDED VR APPLICATIONS

While the list of powerful VR drawing applications is growing all the time, here are a few suggestions for teachers or educators who are new to VR:

- *Tilt Brush VR*—*Tilt Brush* is a room-scale 3D-painting virtual reality application available from Google, initially developed by Skillman & Hackett. According to the *Tilt Brush* website, *Tilt Brush* lets the user paint in 3D space with virtual reality. The room is the canvas. The palette is one's imagination. The possibilities are endless.[3]
- *MasterpieceVR*—This application allows users to sculpt and draw using intuitive, dynamic features. Designers can create models for use in games, animation, digital art, industrial design, and 3D printing. Use reference images or live, in-game web feeds to have art jams with a class or meetup group. Additionally, users can create collaboratively with friends or colleagues, or teach others in real time in the same virtual space.[4]
- *SculptrVR*—*SculptrVR* gives users unlimited space, so their imagination is totally free. This application makes it easy to create, explore, and share brilliant new worlds and sculptures in virtual reality. *SculptrVR* lets users upload their creation to an online gallery or download their object to be 3D printed.[5]

IMPLICATIONS FOR EDUCATORS

In my recent interview with Rosie Summers, an experienced VR artist, workshop leader, and animator, she suggested that new users to VR need to be given some time to explore and discover.[6] After this period of "play," users should be given direction in the form of a small task. For example, she suggested that students be presented with a large Egyptian pyramid and asked to draw one small piece or artefact that would go inside the pyramid. "Some artists get overwhelmed by the openness or vastness of the space and need a sense of context as a starting point."[7]

She also suggested that, when new users are introduced to VR drawing applications for the first time, they be allowed to practice using pallet tools such as the ruler, mirroring, and spray painting tools in advance of creation. Another creative idea or project that could be done with an entire class is the creation of a VR Advent calendar. Each day has a door, and behind the door could be a student-designed artefact. The artefact could be removed and displayed in a virtual world.

Rosie also mentions the efficacy of having students design a small artefact that could then be displayed in a virtual art gallery. To get an idea of what a VR art gallery might look like, please see The Museum of Other Realities, https://museumor.com/. It is a good idea to have students envision their art creations on paper or with plasticine first before getting them to design inside the VR application.

Besides creating VR artefacts, some VR applications allow users to get an idea about issues related to art and design. One such example is *Kingspray Graffiti* VR. This application will enable users to immerse themselves in a city environment and get a sense of what it is like to create graffiti art, without jail time. The concept of whether graffiti is good or bad varies around the world. Allowing students to wrap their heads around this issue by playing *Kingspray Graffiti* is a great way to engage students in deep thinking and discussion. For examples of lesson guides related to art education, please see **Appendix B** at the end of this book.

NOTES

1. "MYP Arts Subject Brief," International Education—International Baccalaureate®, n.d., https://www.ibo.org/globalassets/digital-toolkit/brochures/myp-brief_arts_2015.pdf.
2. Anonymous Grade 10 Student, Personal Interview, Singapore, October 5, 2019.
3. "Tilt Brush on Steam," Welcome to Steam, accessed January 26, 2020, https://store.steampowered.com/app/327140/Tilt_Brush/.
4. "MasterpieceVR," SpringboardVR, accessed January 26, 2020, https://springboardvr.com/marketplace/masterpiecevr.
5. "SculptrVR," SpringboardVR, accessed January 26, 2020, https://springboardvr.com/marketplace/sculptrvr.
6. Rosie Summers, Podcast Interview, https://cfrehlich.podbean.com/e/episode-24-vr-and-art-with-rosie-summers/ December 16, 2019.
7. Summers, "Podcast Interview."

6

VR and Puzzle Games

> VR simulations that engage learners as explorers shift the focus from content acquisition to active inquiry.[1]
>
> —Meredith Thompson

My 16-year-old daughter's birthday was coming up, and as a cool dad who had designed a Harry Potter–themed party, a Minute-To-Win-It party, and a forensics mystery party, there was a lot of pressure to make this one "gold standard." After much research, I decided to take her and her friends to an escape room. The escape room was a Zombie Apocalypse (pause for criticisms based on the inappropriate theme). The story line was that a cannibal had captured us, and nine of us were locked inside three separate cages within a large room.

Inside each metal cage were clues; some were helpful, and others were inconsequential or "red herrings." As a team, we all had to work together to get out of each cage by opening the big lock. Then, once out of the pens, we needed to solve more puzzles to get out of the room before the zombies cooked us for dinner. As crazy as this experience sounds, it remains a favorite memory for my daughter years later.

THE IMPORTANCE OF PROBLEM SOLVING IN EDUCATION

Since the first escape room opened its doors in 2007, the industry has grown to reach most of the world. According to Wikipedia, an escape room is a game in which a team of players cooperatively discover clues, solve puzzles, and accomplish tasks in one or more rooms to progress and achieve a specific goal in a limited amount of time.[2] The goal is often to escape from the site of the game. Escape rooms offer a unique and innovative way to promote valuable critical thinking and problem-solving skills.

Escape rooms allow participants to question, wonder, make comparisons and contrasts, build on theories, examine things from different perspectives, notice, observe, gather, identify, predict, and delve deeply to uncover complexities. It is no wonder escape rooms are so popular in the twenty-first century. Education has also recognized the inherent value of escape room learning. In 2015, James Sanders and Mark Hammon launched Breakout EDU. Breakout EDU is an immersive learning game platform that brings the escape room to the classroom.[3] Since then, thousands of Breakout EDU activities have been designed and launched in classrooms around the world.

THE RISE OF ELASTIC THINKING

Change is an inevitable part of our world and life. Heraclitus, a Greek philosopher, is quoted as saying, "Change is the only constant in life." How people adapt and adjust to change is paramount. In his book *Elastic: Flexible Thinking in a Time of Change*, Leonard Mlodinow describes this adaptation as a way of finding connections to complex problems. How people process information is a big part of his book, where he emphasizes that information processing should be about creating ways to see unfamiliar patterns as new systems.[4] He cautions users to move beyond "autopilot," whereby the brain is fixed to think in one direction.

For example, when one drives to work each day, the mind becomes so accustomed to this pattern that the interrogation of the process fails. It becomes so trivial that the brain does not need to allocate a lot of resources to it anymore. Yet, if people are exposed to a situation in which their brain needs to process a multitude of information and make meaning from this to activate new learning, they become more ready for change. So how do people tune their brain to pay attention to thoughts and ideas that might lead to innovative and creative solutions to problems or puzzles? When faced with a problem, one might be exposed to a host of ideas, some odd and unconventional, and some more conventional.

Alas, brains need to be trained to be able to pivot and change, or focus on one particular path to solve a problem. If one's mind is fixed with a specific filter or way of doing things, then one's ability to solve problems is limited. Pause, contemplation, and meditation can be critical factors in producing elastic thinking and, therefore, superior problem-solving skills.[5] Additionally, practice, reflection, and rumination on our problem-solving abilities can create more elastic thinking.

WHY VR FOR PUZZLE GAMES?

Immersive virtual reality, with its ability to create any kind of environment imaginable, has turned into the perfect medium to design escape room–type puzzles and games for users to stretch their mental problem-solving and critical thinking muscles. In VR, users are not bound by the limitations of the real world, so VR escape rooms and puzzle games can be anything. Like physical escape rooms, VR environments challenge participants to harness the same set of critical thinking skills listed above.

Furthermore, since VR gives users a sense of presence and embodiment, participants can interact with objects in the environment and feel the same emotional response as a real puzzle game or escape room. This connection to the spatial area may provide greater focus and engagement. VR can minimize the uncontrollable distractions that might deter people from the cognitive load needed to think critically and solve puzzles, because users shut out the real world by being inside the HMD.

WHAT FEATURES MAKE SOME PUZZLE GAMES BETTER THAN OTHERS?

A search on the popular VR platform for games, Steam, indicates that there are over 579 different VR puzzle-type games, leaving users with many choices.[6] Although I willingly admit I have not tried all 579 puzzle VR games on Steam, I have tried over 20. From these experiences, here is a summary of a few characteristics that make some better than others. These are three common characteristics of popular VR puzzle games:

- Have an Interesting Story or Narrative—A good story can be exciting and captivating, and when it is weaved within the game plan, it is even more powerful. In a puzzle game, the story or narrative should be subtle and not something that is always at the forefront of the gameplay. It helps weave one level of the game to another like chapters in a book.
- Keep It Simple but Not Too Simple—There is a balance between doing puzzles so easy that the user gets bored and so hard that the user gets frustrated and gives up. Good VR puzzle games find a balance between these two ends of the spectrum.
- Innovative Game Mechanics or Affordances—Finding unique and creative ways for people to interact with the puzzles and clues adds value to the game or application. When VR puzzle games move beyond the mechanics of hiding and seeking evidence to making a special connection to objects through scale and strange interactions, users often delight in the experience. One example of this is the game *A Fisherman's Tale*, which is described below.

RECOMMENDED VR PUZZLE APPLICATIONS

While many puzzle-type VR applications offer characteristics and affordances mentioned above, here are three VR puzzle games that would be fantastic additions to any school or classroom.

- *The Curious Tale of the Stolen Pets*—According to the Steam website, the users will experience an interactive tale of childlike wonder. In this application, users need to help their grandfather solve the mystery of the stolen pets by exploring fantastic miniature worlds crafted from the ground up for VR. Every world is unique, full of interactions and colorful life.[7]
- *A Fisherman's Tale*—In this learning experience, users will practice flexible thinking to solve a VR puzzle game. In this learning experience, users are challenged to bend the laws of physics in order to help Bob, a tiny fisherman puppet, overcome a storm to reach the top of a lighthouse. Playing as Bob, the user lives alone in a tiny cabin, oblivious to the world outside. When their radio broadcasts a storm alert, they have to get to the top of the lighthouse and turn on the light. But as they try to leave their cabin with the help of some uncanny sidekicks, users realize what's waiting outside is not at all what they expected.[8]
- *Form*—Playing as the gifted Dr. Eli, the user has superhuman powers of geometric visualization—the unintended consequence of childhood trauma. The participant can use their powers to follow the signal through The Obelisk and explore dreamlike memories to unlock puzzles in their own mind. This path could lead the player to a new existence … or it could leave them trapped in their past forever.[9]

For examples of lesson guides related to VR problem solving and puzzles, please see **Appendix C** at the end of this book.

NOTES

1. Meredith Thompson et al., "Authenticity, Interactivity, and Collaboration in VR Learning Games," Frontiers, n.d., https://www.frontiersin.org/articles/10.3389/frobt.2018.00133/full#B1.
2. "Escape Room," Wikipedia, the Free Encyclopedia, last modified March 28, 2013, https://en.wikipedia.org/wiki/Escape_room.
3. James Sanders and Mark Hammons, Breakout EDU, n.d., https://www.breakoutedu.com/.
4. Leonard Mlodinow, *Elastic: Flexible Thinking in a Constantly Changing World* (London: Penguin UK, 2018).
5. Mlodinow, *Elastic: Flexible Thinking in a Constantly Changing World*.
6. Valve, "Steam Search," Welcome to Steam, accessed January 26, 2020, https://store.steampowered.com/search/?term=puzzle.
7. Fast Travel Games, "The Curious Tale of the Stolen Pets," Fast Travel Games | Start, accessed January 26, 2020, https://www.fasttravelgames.com/thecurioustaleofthestolenpets/.
8. "A Fisherman's Tale," SpringboardVR, accessed January 26, 2020, https://springboardvr.com/marketplace/afishermanstale.
9. "FORM on Steam," Welcome to Steam, accessed January 26, 2020, https://store.steampowered.com/app/408520/FORM/.

7
VR and the STEM Curriculum

A man's errors are his portals of discovery.

—James Joyce

Inquiry is at the core of an active STEM program. STEM curriculum aims to guide students to independently and collaboratively investigate issues through observation, discovery, and experimentation. Furthermore, connecting experience and explorations to real life is paramount. As students examine various concepts related to STEM, like adaptation, change, and conservation, they will discover the interplay between STEM and ethics, culture, economics, politics, and the environment. With the world seeing a decline in STEM careers, educators must provide a STEM curriculum that sparks interest, curiosity, and passion.[1] Instilling a lifelong desire to tinker, build, solve, hypothesize, calculate, fail, revise, and innovate is the ultimate goal of an effective STEM program.

WHAT IS STEM?

STEM stands for science, technology, engineering, and math. There have been a growing number of STEM courses and classes over the last few years. Many advocates of STEM education believe that these types of programs are essential to keep up with an ever-changing world.[2] A strong STEM program focuses on thinking skills that are common to the four disciplines. Some of these thinking skills are analyzing, problem-solving, innovating, and critical thinking.

Educators need to be cautious when offering STEM classes to ensure they do not erode the nature of STEM. STEM is not meant to be focused on merely learning facts connected to one or more of the disciplines. For example, learning about the parts of a rocket is not STEM education since it is not requiring students to participate in active inquiry, discovery, analysis, and deep thinking. Most STEM programs focus on project-based learning and challenge students to apply their thinking to complex problems. Systems thinking is an essential part of an effective STEM curriculum. Being able to break down complex parts into simpler ones, seeing connections, and adjusting thought processes are all examples of essential STEM thinking skills.

A favorite classroom project as a STEM teacher is having students use the agile thinking skills of learn/try/revise and their understanding of energy and machines to plan and create a Rube Goldberg machine. This hands-on learning activity helps students build conceptual knowledge regarding "systems" as well as content knowledge related to simple machines and the transfer of energy. Additionally, the process of making a Rube Goldberg machine improves student resilience and fortitude through trial and error.

IMPLICATIONS FOR EDUCATORS

Virtual reality can be an excellent tool to facilitate STEM learning and curriculum. Strong STEM programs promote hands-on learning in various disciplines. A robust STEM program requires time-consuming setup and takedown, along with the high cost of specialized equipment and upkeep. Moreover, capital costs for labware and consumable resources like chemicals can be costly. With VR, there is no need to worry about equipment management, and the budget costs can be significantly less compared to the ongoing physical demands of STEM labs. Additionally, as schools accumulate physical resources, there needs to be a place to store everything in the real world. This might be less of a worry with VR equipment.

Besides logistical benefits, virtual reality can also improve STEM pedagogy. Quality STEM programs aspire to connect math, science, and engineering to real-life authentic learning challenges, therefore enhancing engagement, deep thinking, and inspiring students to pursue future STEM careers. Because VR enables designers to create any environment imaginable, connecting STEM learning to real-life simulations and situations is more plausible. Traveling to Mars to test and analyze rock samples for signs of life and designing, testing, and riding one's own roller coaster are just two examples of how VR can connect to authentic real-world learning engagements. Virtual reality can be used to make the impossible, or dangerous, possible. For example, students might want to test the effects of fear on human physiology.

This would not be possible or ethical in the real world. Yet VR can make these types of experiences come true. For example, with a popular VR application by Toast called *Richie's Plank Experience*, students can ride an elevator to the eightieth floor of a tall building and test their fear of heights by walking across a virtual plank. In doing so, students will be able to describe and measure changes in body functions in response to changing conditions. It is important to note that VR isn't meant to be a tool for every STEM topic. VR's most significant utility lies in its ability to transform knowledge. As mentioned earlier in this book, VR is best used to bridge the gap between facts and concepts. It is a medium to experience and interact with the world. VR is "a product to create another world to stimulate curiosity."[3]

RECOMMENDATIONS OF INTERACTIVE STEM APPLICATIONS

There are several outstanding immersive VR applications to support and enhance the STEM skills needed to be successful in an ever-changing world and, more importantly, stretch students' curiosity and innovation.

- *Gadgeteer*—*Gadgeteer* allows students to explore the idea put forth by Aristotle many years ago, "The whole is greater than the sum of its parts." When individual parts are connected to form a complex machine, they are worth more than if the parts were in isolation. In *Gadgeteer*, students can create Rube Goldberg machines with no mess, lost materials, or space needed to store unfinished pieces of work. Balls, tracks, pipes, rectangular prisms, funnels, and other materials are provided in a sandbox-like environment for students to creatively incorporate and transform their ideas into reality.[4]
- *Fantastic Contraption*—Players must build a device or "contraption" that is capable of transporting a jelly ball object from point A to B. Players have free rein when designing their contraptions, so trial and error and experimentation play a major role in this learning experience. Students explore energy transfer, structural balance, and stability. Design thinking skills are put to the test in this wonderful application. As students build, test, and rebuild, they learn to be resilient, and failure is part of the process.[5]
- *Robo Co*—This fun STEM game challenges students to design and build robots that have to complete hapless tasks for a family of humans. Users assemble robots piece by piece, rigging each creation with motors, gears, and customizable wireless controls in order to conquer tricky, open-ended challenge courses. Students will learn how parts and systems work together individually and as a whole.[6]

For examples of lesson guides related to STEM education, please see **Appendix D** at the end of this book.

NOTES

1. "New Research Shows Declining Interest in STEM," Government Technology State & Local Articles—E.Republic, last modified June 11, 2018, https://www.govtech.com/education/k-12/New-Research-Shows-Declining-Interest-in-STEM.html.

2. Anne David, "The Push For STEM Education: Why It Matters," TeachThought, last modified April 16, 2019, https://www.teachthought.com/education/the-push-for-stem-education-why-it-matters/.

3. Jaron Lanier, *Dawn of the New Everything: Encounters with Reality and Virtual Reality* (New York: Henry Holt and Company, 2017).

4. Gadgeteer | Build Your Dream Machine, accessed January 26, 2020, https://gadgeteergame.com/.

5. "Fantastic Contraption," SpringboardVR, accessed January 26, 2020, https://springboardvr.com/marketplace/fantasticcontraption.

6. RoboCo Dev Blog, last modified March 29, 2019, https://roboco.co/.

8
VR and Storytelling

> The purpose of a storyteller is not to tell you how to think, but to give you questions to think upon.
>
> —Brandon Sanderson

According to the International Baccalaureate Language and Literature Subject Guide, the language and literature department is the epicenter of narrative and storytelling content within a school. Through writing and narrative studies, teachers inspire students to be better communicators. Moreover, a substantial literature curriculum aspires to have students interact with chosen text and nontext stories to generate insight into moral, social, economic, political, cultural, and environmental factors.[1] As students experience narratives, they grow to realize that through critical consumption of these stories, they become more aware of their place in the world. Inquiry and conceptual understanding should be a clear goal when exploring narratives by providing students with opportunities to independently and collaboratively investigate, take action, and reflect on a variety of genres.

Good stories move people and have profound effects. The ultimate goal of storytelling is to touch the hearts and minds of people. Traditional stories follow a linear plot, and as the story unfolds, the author carefully reveals essential details about the situation and characters. Readers may passively engage in the narrative. The storyteller uses creative language and exciting plot twists to capture attention and emotionally draw in the audience.

VR STORYTELLING IS DIFFERENT

Storytelling in VR can be quite different. In VR, the viewer is no longer a passive participant. Virtual reality offers the viewer greater access to the environment where the story is taking place. The participant can be part of the story. VR gives the viewer a sense of presence and agency. As the story unfolds, the viewer can look around in different directions within the scene and can play a more active role in the story narrative. With the use of controllers, the viewer might grab and manipulate objectives within the story. Some refer to this new sense of immersion as "story-living" instead of storytelling.

What impact does this new medium have on creating a heightened sense of empathy for the viewer? Chris Milk, an American immersive artist and storyteller, believes that VR is an empathy machine. "The promise that VR can hold is that it's the democratization of human experience," Milk said. "Much like the Internet was the democratization of data."[2] In his 2015 TED talk, Milk spoke about several reasons why VR is such a powerful medium to communicate a story. He proclaims that VR stories can connect people like never before and change people's perception. While VR is still a machine, it is through this machine that people become more connected, compassionate, and empathetic, and more fundamentally, they learn more about what it means to be human.[3]

However, this medium is not without its challenges. There is a delicate balance between giving the viewer too much agency and interactivity, and too little. If the viewer is overwhelmed by engagement, they may not fully understand the plot and characters of a story. On the other hand, too much passivity might create an underwhelming experience, leaving the viewer disappointed. Finding this balance depends on the account. When a VR storyteller lacks unlimited control over the plot, then new techniques need to be employed to get the attention of the viewer. Having a hand controller vibrate at strategic times and positioning sounds are just two possible strategies to trigger viewers to pay attention to certain parts of the story in VR. Ultimately, people won't understand if they don't pay attention.

RECOMMENDED VR NARRATIVES

Below are several examples of VR storytelling narratives that would provide compelling learning for any school or student.

- *Manifest 99*—*Manifest 99* is an ominous and eerie VR story set on a train rumbling through the afterlife. Accompanied by a murder of crows and four mysterious travel companions, the user must uncover the reason why they—and the companions—are on this train travelling into the great beyond. The user can gaze into the eyes of the characters and discover the remnants of their weary souls before they pass on. As participants learn more about the personae of the characters, they feel a stronger sense of connection. In this unique experience, students can analyze the impact of the author's choices regarding how characters are introduced and developed in a narrative. Staring into their eyes helps us wonder and speculate about their past.[4]

- *Firebird La Peri*—In *Firebird La Peri* participants will experience a story told with the immersive power of VR. *La Péri* is based on the music of a one-act ballet of the same name by French composer Paul Dukas and tells the story of Iskender, an aging Magi who seeks the Flower of Immortality for La Peri. There are interactive elements in this narrative and the use of light and sound to enhance presence within the narrative. In this story, perspective-taking is paramount. Perspective is the position from which users observe situations, objects, facts, ideas, and opinions. Different perspectives may lead to multiple representations and interpretations. In virtual reality, the viewer is allowed to explore, look around, and gaze in multiple locations to establish a variety of perspectives. Does this new ability enhance or diminish the audience's imperative (meaning and message of the story or narrative)?[5]
- *Crow: The Legend*—The story of the Rainbow Crow is a Lenape legend, focusing on the concepts of sacrifice and commitment. After a long period of cold weather, the animals of the community become worried. They decide to send a messenger to the Great Sky Spirit to ask for relief. Native Americans are predominantly oral storytellers. They use narratives in the form of legends to pass down important beliefs, customs, and values—especially as they relate to nature and the land. The medium of VR does an effective job of passing on important cultural values evident in the story.[6]

IMPLICATIONS FOR EDUCATORS

Teachers want students to engage in stories and narratives and "lean in" to the learning. As immersive stories advance, more and more of them are becoming highly interactive. Students can be heroes of their own stories. Instead of having participants be passive observers of VR stories and content, VR tools can excite them by being part of the story. Why watch a character in a story, when a user can be the character? This new sense of agency, whereby users are in the story, heightens the connection and emotional attachment to the narrative. Understanding story themes, perspectives, and points of view when the participant is in the story can enhance interest and engagement.

The Under Presents by Tender Claws is one example of a VR narrative that explores the synergy between narrative theater and audience control and agency. It is an entertaining multiplayer experience set between two worlds: a lively vaudeville stage and an intriguing survival narrative.[7] The user will discover the story of a ship stranded in time as supplies dwindle day by day. The participant will follow the characters' interlocking fates. In this part story, part game, the participant can generate magic, play with time, and see cross sections of the ship thanks to a mask they are given in the first scene. It also includes live actors within the narrative to add a sense of unpredictability and authenticity to the experience.

For examples of lesson guides related to storytelling and narratives, please see **Appendix E** at the end of this book.

NOTES

1. "MYP Language and Literature Subject Brief," IBO, accessed January 26, 2020, https://www.ibo.org/globalassets/digital-toolkit/brochures/myp-brief_language-literature_2015.pdf.

2. Lucas Matney, "Vrse CEO Chris Milk Talks VR Storytelling and the Road to Virtual Reality's Citizen Kane—TechCrunch," TechCrunch, last modified May 10, 2016, https://techcrunch.com/2016/05/10/vrse-ceo-chris-milk-talks-vr-storytelling-and-the-road-to-virtual-realitys-citizen-kane/.

3. Chris Milk, "How Virtual Reality Can Create the Ultimate Empathy Machine," TED: Ideas Worth Spreading, last modified March 7, 2015, https://www.ted.com/talks/chris_milk_how_virtual_reality_can_create_the_ultimate_empathy_machine.

4. "Manifest 99," SpringboardVR, accessed January 26, 2020, https://springboardvr.com/marketplace/manifest99.

5. "Firebird—La Peri," SpringboardVR, accessed January 26, 2020, https://springboardvr.com/marketplace/firebirdlaperi.

6. "Crow: The Legend," SpringboardVR, accessed January 26, 2020, https://springboardvr.com/marketplace/thecrow.

7. Jesse Damiani, "'The Under Presents? Is a Novel Exploration of VR and Live Immersive Theatre," Forbes, last modified November 22, 2019, https://www.forbes.com/sites/jessedamiani/2019/11/19/the-under-presents-is-a-novel-exploration-of-vr-and-live-immersive-theatre/#9efa04874556.

9

VR for Health and Wellness

Sitting is the new smoking.

—Dr. Levine

As VR continues to increase in popularity in the next few years, many opponents to this emerging technology worry that it is going to increase the problem of sedentarism and "couch potato syndrome" that already plagues many of our youth who are addicted to video games. Is VR really that bad for our health and wellness? According to the Virtual Reality Institute for Health and Exercise, "For 20 years video games have had a negative connotation in the health and fitness community. The stereotype of the unhealthy, antisocial gamer that hides in the basement and has no friends has long been untrue."[1] Especially as it pertains to VR. Thanks to room-scale technology whereby the HMD can be tracked in defined space, users of VR can get up off the couch, move around, and be active. "Robert Long, of Maryland, said he used VR games to improve his health and to lose more than 100 pounds after years of managing pain resulting from two car accidents."[2]

WHAT IS HEALTH AND WELLNESS?

According to the International Baccalaureate Physical Education Guide, a robust physical education, health, and wellness curriculum aims to inspire students to take an active role in keeping the body healthy mentally, physically, and socially. Physical education and wellness means learning about and learning through movement related to the body and mind. Effective athletic programs promote a balance of activities and experiences for students to see that being active and healthy is a state of being.[3] When appropriately implemented, physical education and wellness courses instill self-efficacy, positivity, confidence, and engagement. Being healthy is a central idea of what it means to be human. By being exposed to a variety of different sports and experiences, students build a strong understanding of how to thrive in a global society.

WHY VR AND HEALTH AND WELLNESS?

VR can have a significant role in enhancing and supplementing a robust physical education and wellness program. Here are several reasons why VR works well with this discipline:

- Activity Is Key—The award-winning VR application *Beat Saber* has sold over 1 million copies. The simple premise behind *Beat Saber* is that the user must dodge walls and slice cubes with a handheld saber. It requires the user to get out of their chair and move their body in different directions while swinging their arms. Dr. Kern from the Virtual Reality Institute of Health and Exercise claims that when working out with *Beat Saber* "players burn 6 to 8 calories per minute. Boxing games, which involve quick jabs and hops, dominate the top categories. They usually burn between 6 and 10 calories a minute."[4] There are well over 30 types of VR exercise applications available to users today, and this list keeps growing.
- Increase in Motivation—One of the hardest hurdles to regular exercise is just doing it. The lack of motivation to commit to daily activity is the number one reason why many people fall out of the habit when it comes to adopting an exercise routine. With VR, a user can break the monotony associated with exercise. There are endless opportunities for varying the type of training and environment. VR can trick the brain into thinking that exercise is enjoyable. When a user puts on a VR headset, they block the distractions of the real world, allowing them to focus and concentrate on the activity. Additionally, many VR applications enhance motivation through gamification. Turning exercise into a subtle competition can help keep people interested in working out for more extended periods.
- Access to a Variety of Sports and Virtual Equipment—Providing access to a variety of different sports to cater to the needs and interests of a wide group of students in school is a daunting task. Yet if schools want students to be active, they need to be able to differentiate their physical education programs. Offering traditional sports like volleyball, basketball, and soccer is fine for some, but what about the students who are not interested in these types of sports? VR can provide this kind of latitude. Moreover, the costs of providing the necessary physical equipment, space, and upkeep can be huge. For example, tennis courts take up a lot of space. With VR, the cost is substantially lower.

VR for Health and Wellness

- Accessible to People with Disabilities—Many VR applications can be played by people who have injuries or physical disabilities. For example, people in a wheelchair can still play VR tennis because the artificial intelligence (AI) in the applications tracks the ball and moves the user close to the ball so that all the participant has to worry about is the arm swing.
- Mental Wellness—Schools are starting to realize that helping students cope with mental health is an essential piece of the learning puzzle. Students who have a healthy level of mental stability learn better. Helping students navigate the stressful game of life is not easy. The state in which students are calm, reflective, introspective, still, mentally focused, and present in the moment is often called "mindfulness." There are a plethora of mindful techniques like yoga and meditation to foster this state in students. VR can be a valuable tool to promote mindfulness and mental wellness in students. For example, *Nature Treks* is an application that allows students to explore a variety of tranquil environments peacefully. Students might don a headset and walk or sit calmly in a forest.

RECOMMENDATIONS FOR HEALTH AND WELLNESS VR APPLICATIONS

- *Where Thoughts Go*[5]—This application builds on a student's mental health and wellness. Sharing intimate thoughts, feelings, and emotions can be very cathartic but not always easy in the real world without the help of a trusted professional psychiatrist. What if VR could provide affordances that engender a safe place for students to do this? Can immersive VR offer emotional release and growth through thoughtful introspection? *Where Thoughts Go* aims to give users a safe space free from trolling, negativity, and judgment to allow users to share audio experiences based on provocative questions about life. By the end of the VR experience, the user may become more self-aware of their journey in life.
- *Audioshield*[6]—Getting regular exercise for some people can be a struggle because it sometimes makes them uncomfortable when they push the physiological limits of their body. Having a distraction like listening to podcasts, watching television, a movie, or participating with others in a group can sometimes distract people from the pain and discomfort induced by exercise. Some immersive VR applications have been designed to make users active during game-play. In these situations, painless minutes pass by without users' brains even knowing that their heart rates have increased. *Audioshield* is a fast-paced game that challenges the user to block the beats. *Audioshield* puts the user at the point of impact for every hit in the songs. Participants block incoming orbs with shields and move around in the process. Can an active VR application like *Audioshield* increase users' enjoyment of exercise while still maintaining a high enough threshold of activity to qualify as regular exercise?

- *Hoops VR*[7]—Learning a new sport requires focus, practice, refinement, and reflection. Skill development does not usually happen automatically. However, with the right emphasis on technique, body positioning, and transfer of energy, beginners can hone their skills and become better at any sport. In this VR application, users will reflect on their basketball shooting skills. *Hoops VR* is specially designed so participants can live out the ultimate basketball free-throw challenge.

For examples of lesson guides related to physical education and health curriculum, please see **Appendix F** at the end of this book.

NOTES

1. "About Us—Virtual Reality Institute of Health and Exercise," n.d., https://vrhealth.institute/about/.

2. Signe Brewster, "Virtual Reality Video Games that Double as Exercise," *The New York Times*—Breaking News, World News & Multimedia, last modified September 20, 2019, https://www.nytimes.com/2019/09/17/smarter-living/wirecutter/virtual-reality-video-games-that-double-as-exercise.html.

3. "MYP Physical Education and Health Subject Brief," International Education—International Baccalaureate®, n.d., https://www.ibo.org/globalassets/digital-toolkit/brochures/myp-brief_phys-health-ed_2015.pdf.

4. Brewster, "Virtual Reality Games that Double as Exercise."

5. "Where Thoughts Go," SpringboardVR, accessed January 26, 2020, https://springboardvr.com/marketplace/wherethoughtsgo.

6. "Audioshield," SpringboardVR, accessed January 26, 2020, https://springboardvr.com/marketplace/audioshield.

7. "Hoops VR," SpringboardVR, accessed January 26, 2020, https://springboardvr.com/marketplace/hoopsvr.

10

VR and Social Studies

> A mind once opened never closes.
>
> —Anonymous

There are several reasons to stay on top of the news and develop a critical pallet as an informed citizen in our world today. Fake news, unethical use of voter data, and fears of automation are just a few hot topics prevalent in media. There is no shortage of current events in the news today. According to the International Baccalaureate MYP Individuals and Societies Subject Guide, a robust social studies curriculum encourages learners to respect and understand the world around them. Individuals need the necessary skills to provocate and inquire into geographical, historical, political, social, economic, technological, and cultural factors that have an impact on society.[1]

Social studies teachers aim to help students connect their evolving identities to global issues and fundamentally inquire into the complex topic of what it means to be human. Furthermore, teaching students to be responsible citizens within local and global communities helps them participate in meaningful ways to make a difference. This focus and interplay of thoughts and ideas needs to be discovery-based and highly experiential. If teachers want students to be empathetic toward the world and believe that other people with their differences can be "right," then they need to know what it is like to be in another's shoes. The world is a prominent and complex place, and having an international mindset is key to peace and harmony.

WHY VR FOR SOCIAL STUDIES?

There are several reasons why virtual reality is a great tool to enhance a social studies curriculum. Here are some important considerations:

- Fostering Empathy and Understanding—This book has already discussed how VR, with its powerful immersion, embodiment, and sense of "presence," can transform people's perspectives. Walking a mile in someone else's shoes is possible with VR. For example, Stanford University developed a VR application titled *Becoming Homeless*.[2] In this highly interactive experience, the user plays the role of what it would be like to have one's resources diminished to the point where the user was living on the street. I have personally watched many students go through this experience, and the reaction is transformative for most. One anonymous twelfth-grade girl commented, "I used to be scared of homeless people on the street until I experienced this VR application. Now, I have more respect for their situation."[3] There are many topics within humanities that merit the attention of VR developers to create empathetic VR experiences like *Becoming Homeless*. The United Nations has recognized the power of VR. "Since January 2015, the UN SDG Action Campaign has coordinated the United Nations Virtual Reality Series to bring the world's most pressing challenges home to decision-makers and global citizens around the world, pushing the bounds of empathy. Also, the UN SDG Action Campaign is exploring opportunities to expand United Nations Virtual Reality's (UNVR's) use as an educational tool."[4]
- Virtual Field Trips—Whether classes are studying ancient Rome or what Berlin looked and felt like before the Berlin wall came down, virtual reality has the power to recreate history like never before. Thanks to creative and imaginative programmers, developers, and historians, VR can help students understand what it was like in a particular time and place. This is akin to a time machine. Although their experiences are still at the early stages, it will be vital to consider interactivity as they develop and evolve. Passivity and looking around in 360 degrees can be done using two-dimensional computers. If VR is to bring historical, present, and future events to life to create deeper understanding, active experiences are vital.
- Virtual Simulations for Social Studies Concepts—Many students in the world live in large cities. And one thing that is shocking about urban youth is their lack of understanding about how to grow things. Farming is a foreign concept to most. Since the majority of the world population lives in dense urban dwellings, there is little room for gardens. How are schools to teach sustainability when many students do not even have a clue how to grow food? Enter VR. VR can have students understanding and experiencing what it is like to be a farmer who provides for others. Students could enter a VR application and be in charge of tending the soil, planting the seeds, irrigating the crop, and finally harvesting. Or, a good simulation might also consider exposing the farmer to

a water shortage or soil infertility and have participants deal with and adapt to these hard realities that sometimes exist in farming. The possibilities of virtual simulations to aid in understanding critical cultural, geographical, political, and economic scenarios around the world are bountiful. What would it feel like to be in a political protest? What does political debate look like in the parliament in countries like Singapore that have only had one ruling party in their history?

RECOMMENDATIONS FOR VR APPLICATIONS

While the list of immersive, engaging, and thought-provoking VR applications continues to grow, here are some recommendations for educators:

- *Becoming Homeless*[5]—Stanford VR's *"Becoming Homeless"* invites students to understand and empathize with the rights and responsibilities surrounding homelessness. This engaging and interactive narrative puts the participant in the shoes of a homeless person. The user learns firsthand how and what it is like to end up on the street. The user has to experience selling their possessions to ward off eviction, sleeping in their car only to be approached by the police, and living on a bus where a man tries to steal their backpack. The ultimate goal is for participants to speculate over who is at fault for the problem of homelessness around the world.
- *The Blu*[6]—Can immersive VR help us build relationships with nature? Thousands of people around the world spend money to go to view wildlife in its natural habitat. Is this a sustainable practice? Are ecotours doing more harm than good? Take whale-watching, for example. With the boat gas pollution and danger of having a negative encounter with the whales, is whale-watching really helping the whales? Could there be a more environmentally friendly alternative? What about immersive VR? *The Blu* offers users a close-up encounter with whales and other ocean life. Experience the wonder and majesty of the ocean through a series of habitats and come face to face with some of the most awe-inspiring species on the planet. Is this the new ecotourism?
- *Cave Digger*[7]—Mining used to be a fun and lucrative profession during the "gold rush" days when minerals like gold were readily available above ground. Aboveground mining or placer mining was safe and inexpensive. Nowadays, most precious minerals are found deep below the surface of the earth. Underground mining can be a hard life. Explosions and poor air quality are just two reasons why underground mining is so difficult. In this VR experience, the user will play the role of an underground miner and explore and discover the world of mining. Gear up with numerous unique tools and explore the town and the depths of the mountain. What does it take to become rich as a miner? Is the reward worth the risk?

For lesson guides related to social studies curriculum, please see **Appendix G** at the end of this book.

NOTES

1. "MYP Individuals and Society Subject Brief," International Education—International Baccalaureate®, n.d., https://www.ibo.org/globalassets/digital-toolkit/brochures/myp-brief_individuals-societies_2015.pdf.

2. "Becoming Homeless: A Human Experience," VHIL, accessed January 26, 2020, https://vhil.stanford.edu/becominghomeless/.

3. Anonymous Grade 12 Student, Personal Interview, Singapore December 13, 2019.

4. UN Virtual Reality—United Nations Virtual Reality (UNVR), a project implemented by the UN SDG Action Campaign, n.d., http://unvr.sdgactioncampaign.org/.

5. "Becoming Homeless: A Human Experience."

6. "TheBlu: Season 1 (Home Edition)," SpringboardVR, accessed January 26, 2020, https://springboardvr.com/marketplace/thebluhome.

7. "Cave Digger," SpringboardVR, accessed January 26, 2020, https://springboardvr.com/marketplace/cavedigger.

Conclusion

> The goal of education is for learners to *leave the VR space with new concepts embedded in their ever-changing knowledge structures.*[1]
>
> —Mina C. Johnson-Glenberg

LET'S GO FLY A KITE

Some people have described a kite as "happiness on a string." A colorful kite with its long well-decorated tail is a beautiful thing to behold in the sky. The long tail of the kite with its various ribbons helps provide the balance needed by the kite to navigate the winds. Readers who have flown a kite before will know how important it is to have a windy day to get the kite off the ground to fly high in the sky. The wind provides a launching pad for the kite to twist, turn, dive, and explore. What a joy it is to hold the kite string and skilfully navigate so that the kite remains in the air for a fulfilling experience. The thrill comes from the unpredictable tugs and twists endured and the notion that adaptation to the grip on the string ensures the kite does not come crashing down.

Immersive VR experiences are like flying a kite. In this metaphor, the student is the kite exploring and discovering the open skies. Like the unpredictability of soaring on a windy day, well-designed conceptual VR experiences allow students to make meaning of their surroundings. As educators, it is our responsibility to hold the string and carefully guide the student along the journey. With each flight, the student grows in confidence, skill, and has a deeper understanding of the world. Making VR magical can be accomplished through well-thought-out CRISP lesson guides to ensure students do not come crashing to the ground as a result of their VR experience. The colorful tails of the kite represent the various concepts or "big ideas" and skills students have mastered as they devour VR applications and learn to internalize conceptual understanding, bringing balance to their education. The longer the tail, the more prepared the student is for an ever-changing world.

DO NOT SETTLE FOR MEDIOCRITY

> We are shaped by our experiences but through learning we have the power to choose the experiences that are more fulfilling in order to shape our destiny.[2]
>
> —Kay Peterson and David A. Kolb

VR is currently going through a bit of a honeymoon period. Most new users are easily fascinated by any experience. But, as our "taste buds" evolve, the demand for content that is truly immersive and interactive will increase. A large number of educational VR experiences are far too passive. The user puts on an HMD and views material from all angles and close up, similar to 360-degree videos offered on YouTube. For example, tours through virtual museums and artefacts only provide a basic level of interactivity. While this new visual perspective might enhance learning and understanding, over time, due to its lack of engagement, students will get bored. Users need to have active experiences and heighten control or agency. Paller and Voss did a study on how curiosity and memory were different in passive versus active tasks. In the study participants were asked to recall a series of pictures.[3]

In the first group, the pictures were scrolled across the screen and the viewer had no control over the sequence. In the second group, participants were given greater control and agency. They were able to change the direction and order of the pictures and could click on them. Paller and Voss found that there was a heightened sense of curiosity and memory recall from the more active second group.[4] A "killer" app for education needs to ignite the brain and provide a powerful learning experience that will be both memorable and remarkable. Powerful VR applications invite users to think conceptually by asking them to physically manipulate and engage in the material to develop twenty-first-century learning skills. "[C]reate experiences that don't require narrative, or the presentation of facts, at all. If we want to unlock the potential of VR learning fully, the lesson should emerge from the experience as an active process of discovery."[5]

In a TEDx talk by Dr. Michael Roussel, he discusses how surprise activates the brain to instill stronger connections to learning.[6] Dr. Roussel talks about our physiological and neurological responses when we are surprised about something. Physiologically, a person's eyes might open wider and his heart might speed up. Furthermore, the brain will often release a chemical called dopamine. When such a response occurs, people are ready to form new beliefs and reshape their old ones. "For example, if one walks outside to go cut his lawn and sees a zebra eating grass in the front yard, he would certainly be surprised. As a result, the brain starts to process the information, thanks to a rush of a chemical in our brain called dopamine."[7]

Conclusion

Dopamine is a brain chemical motivator that signals people to pay attention because something important is happening.

For our ancestors, surprise usually meant danger or a great opportunity. Dr. Roussel believes that in a moment of surprise people are hardwired to learn instantly. As the event plays out, people start to evaluate whether it is positive or negative. It is like someone's attention is hijacked. The dopamine makes people curious about what just happened and fuels their search for information.

So, if surprise is so important in learning, can it be operationalized and strategically used to evoke powerful learning in VR? The answer to this is an obvious yes! Here are a few ways to evoke a surprise event that might stimulate learning in VR:

- The Strategic Use of Haptics—Haptics in virtual reality refers to the science of applying touch (tactile) sensation and controls interaction. Most commonly, these are created through the vibration and buzzing of the hand controllers. More importantly, haptics can help generate an element of surprise, which may enhance our learning of an event or experience when triggered strategically. For example, the VR application *Feed a Titanosaur* is an educational experience in which users are given the opportunity to grab a branch from a tree and offer it up to a giant Titanosaur. As the participant puts food into the dinosaur's mouth, a buzzing is triggered on one of the controllers, surprising the user. This event may help participants to understand and realize what it's like to feed a giant dinosaur, and the sheer size and scale of the organism is embedded in one's cognitive psyche. The physical buzzing of the hand controller releases dopamine in the user's brain to trigger them to pay attention.
- The Strategic Use of Sound—Auditory messages and cues can have a profound cognitive effect on beliefs and memories. Songs and sounds are often associated with positive or negative life moments. For example, whenever one hears the song "Drive" by the Cars, they may remember their first slow dance. Sounds can act as a surprise mechanism to help trigger a response that may evoke learning. Take the highly popular game *Beat Saber*. The game requires the user to strike blocks in certain directions with their handheld saber. In this VR application, the body works in tune with the gameplay, enabling it to act in the harmonic, rhythmic, or melodic form to the background music. The sounds of the song act as a trigger mechanism. As a user dodges walls and slices cubes with the saber, he starts to feel a stronger connection with the game. The timing and rhythmic flow of the songs help release dopamine, which creates a positive connection to the game. This interplay becomes motivating.

Surprise as a tool to trigger learning episodes is not new to education. Those who studied to become a teacher back in the 1990s remember the work of Madeline Hunter and her research on lesson design.[8] Dr. Hunter proclaimed that good lesson plans begin with a "hook" or anticipatory set. This trigger event heightened students' curiosity and engagement.

A popular "go-to" strategy was the "mystery bag." This was a pillowcase populated with items that might connect with the rest of the lesson and learning outcomes. Students would have to stick their hand into the mystery bag without seeing inside and guess the item. If they were correct, the class would talk about how it would relate to the lesson experiences in the next hour.

As VR starts to mature in the educational landscape, educators need to seek out "mystery bag" type experiences. When evaluating and using VR applications, look for encounters that evoke surprise, build connections, and trigger learning through strategic haptics and audio.

WHERE DO EDUCATORS GO FROM HERE?

The Appendix part of this book provides readers with several examples of VR lesson guides, which can be used by teachers to navigate students before, during, and after their VR experiences. Careful consideration was taken to ensure the guides provide students with a deep understanding of big ideas and concepts that make learning more relevant and engaging.

ACKNOWLEDGMENTS

I want to thank SpringboardVR, who owns the intellectual property associated with these lesson guides, to allow these materials to be included in this book for educators. It is my goal for educators around the world to lower any barriers to implementing VR in education, and increase interactive VR conceptual learning in schools.

NOTES

1. Mina C. Johnson-Glenberg, "Immersive VR and Education: Embodied Design Principles that Include Gesture and Hand Controls," *Frontiers in Robotics and AI* 5 (2018).
2. Kay Peterson and David A. Kolb, *How You Learn Is How You Live: Using Nine Ways of Learning to Transform Your Life* (Oakland: Berrett-Koehler Publishers, 2017).
3. Ken A. Paller and Joel L. Voss, "Accurate Recognition Based on Explicit Versus Implicit Memory," *PsycEXTRA Dataset*, 2008.
4. Paller and Voss, "Accurate Recognition Based on Explicit VR Implicit Memory."
5. Jeremy Bailenson, *Experience on Demand: What Virtual Reality Is, How It Works, and What It Can Do* (New York: W. W. Norton & Company, 2018).
6. Michael Rousell, Michael Rousell—The Power of Surprise, last modified November 30, 2018, http://michaelrousell.com/.
7. Rousell, "The Power of Surprise."
8. "Madeline Hunter Lesson Plan Model," The Second Principle, last modified May 31, 2014, https://thesecondprinciple.com/essential-teaching-skills/models-of-teaching/madeline-hunter-lesson-plan-model/.

Appendix A

VR Lesson Guides for Cooperative Learning and Communication

Lesson Guide: Cooperation and Working as a Team
Acron: Attack of the Squirrels VR
Designed by Craig Frehlich B.Ed., M.Ed.

© 2019 Springboard Virtual Reality, Inc.

Target Age:	Target Subject/Field:	Essential Idea:
10- Adult, Grade 5 and up	Interdisciplinary, Advisor/ Communication Skills, Teamwork, Group skills	How can we work effectively with others?

Goal of the Learning Application:
We have all heard the saying, "Two heads are better than one" and "it takes a village to raise a mountain." Working effectively as a team is an essential part of society. Alas, group dynamics can be tricking, but with explicit practice, people can improve their skills. Acron: Attack of the Squirrels is a modern-day version of capture the flag. In this multiplayer experience, one player in VR takes on the role of a large, ancient tree that is the sole protector of the golden acorns. Meanwhile, two to eight frenemies can then grab their iOS and Android devices to become rebel squirrels that will do anything to steal the golden acorns using an arsenal of unique abilities. Cooperation and strategy amongst the team of squirrels are paramount.

Possible Learning Objectives:	Key Concepts & Vocabulary:
• Students will be able to learn how to give and receive meaningful feedback effectively. • Students will be able to exercise leadership and take on various roles within a group. • Students will be able to delegate and share responsibility for decision making. • Students will be able to listen actively to other perspectives and ideas. • Students will be able to develop strategies to improve communication within a group.	• Non-verbal communication • Verbal communication • Effective communication • Leadership Skills • Group Skills

Pre-Application Guidelines & Questions:
Before entering the VR application, users should answer the following questions.
- Have a look at this video, https://www.youtube.com/watch?v=6HfBbSUORvo. What is the moral or message of the animated short?

Appendix A 47

- Working collaboratively is not as easy as it sounds. Search the internet and list three crucial tips to make group work more effective.
- Every group often has a leader. Ants have a queen, sports teams usually have a captain, and some countries have a president. What are some roles of the leader in the group? Besides the leader, what are some other group roles?
- Watch this video, https://www.youtube.com/watch?v=r3c7uAJRx3U. Summarize by listing three critical points to consider about teams and leadership.

Important Tips & Tricks to Consider Inside this VR Application

What to expect? Students should be put into groups, 3-9 people. One person should put on the VR headset and become the tree while the rest of the students should download the Acron app from the Apple or Google Play store. Before playing, the students will need to pick a type of squirrel. Here are the different squirrel characters:

- The marmots are a much easier target, being slower and much larger, but can employ a portable shield that'll protect them from projectiles before it's worn down.
- The red squirrels are small and fast and can activate a sprint ability that makes them run even faster for a short burst.
- The ground squirrels are the smallest and can dig tunnels and travel underground.
- Chipmunks can build ramps and bridges that are especially useful for levels with water or lava.

Round 1- Random. Allow students to pick whatever character they want and encourage them to play as an independent. Play a few rounds like this and encourage students to switch between characters.

Round 2- Get students to team up in groups of two or three. Each group must be the same character, and all characters should be represented in the game. Play a couple of rounds like this.

Round 3- All students are the same character, and someone is designated the captain of the team or the leader. The leader needs to act as the quarterback who calls out plays. Play a couple of rounds like this.

Post-Application Guidelines & Reflections

Once the student/user has explored and navigated through the VR experience, they should answer the following questions:

- Which round was most enjoyable for you? Why?
- Which round was the least enjoyable for you? Why?
- Of the different types of characters, which one do you think has the best properties or characteristics to be successful at the game?
- Verbal and non-verbal communication is essential while playing. Give some examples of verbal and non-verbal communication skills that were used during the game-play.

- Was playing with a team more effective than when everyone was on their own in round 1?
- Was leadership effective in doing well in the game? Explain.
- What are some of the limitations to these simulations as a way of seeing if group work or leadership is better to accomplish a goal than on your own?

Extension Activities

- Have students watch the movie, Coach Carter, the trailer can be found here, https://www.youtube.com/watch?v=znyAnWUYf2g. Write a report about what lessons can be learnt about playing on a team.
- Go over the rules to the game, capture the flag, which can be found here, https://www.youtube.com/watch?v=Ll0lAy9YX8g. Take students outside and play capture the flag.

Lesson Guide: Effective Decision-Making Under Pressure

Black Hat Cooperative VR

Designed by Craig Frehlich B.Ed., M.Ed.

© 2019 Springboard Virtual Reality, Inc.

Target Age: 10- Adult, Grade 5 and up	Target Subject/Field: Interdisciplinary, Advisor/Decision-making skills, Communication Skills	Essential Idea: How can people collaborate effectively through two-way communication to reach a common goal?

Goal of the Learning Application:
Cooperation requires a shared understanding of how decisions are made and implemented. Active collaboration may be accomplished through clear communication skills and agreed-upon norms. However, just like any skill, this requires explicit practice. In this VR application, we push our decision making and communication skills to the limit. This cooperative game involves two or more people. One player is in VR, sneaking past enemies and collecting treasure. Other players are on the computer and keyboard with access to a full view of the map and hacking superpowers. This game requires quick thinking, trust, effective two-way communication, and unflappable decision-making techniques.

Possible Learning Objectives:	Key Concepts & Vocabulary:
• Students will be able to learn how to give and receive meaningful feedback effectively. • Students will be able to delegate and share responsibility for decision-making. • Students will be able to learn how to help others succeed. • Students will be able to negotiate ideas and information with peers. • Students will be able to develop strategies to improve communication within a group.	• Non-verbal communication • Verbal communication • Effective communication • Decision Making Skills • Leadership Skills

Appendix A

Pre-Application Guidelines & Questions:
Before entering the VR application, users should answer the following questions.
- Watch this video, https://www.youtube.com/watch?v=vPXKJ_9x6aU. Why is having clear and concise communication skills essential for being an Air Traffic Controller?
- Why is being an Air Traffic Controller such a stressful job?
- Research and list three tips for effective communication when under pressure.
- Besides being an Air Traffic Controller, list some other careers that require a person to have a high level of communication skills while under pressure. Why are they so stressful?
- Decision making or leadership styles also apply when it comes to communicating toward a common goal. Have a look at this article and summarize the three techniques listed in the article. https://www.forbes.com/sites/davidcarlin/2019/10/18/democratic-authoritarian-laissez-faire-what-type-of-leader-are-you/#3d44706f2a6b.

Important Tips & Tricks to Consider Inside this VR Application

What to expect? When you launch Black Hat Cooperative, one student will be required to don the HMD, and the other player or players will need to look at the computer display. The student in the HMD will not be able to see the map or other features like laser gates. It is the job of the students outside the VR headset to communicate, guide and lead the student through the map to gather treasure. Students should take turns being inside the headset. Additionally, students should experiment with different types of communication/decision-making/leadership styles.

Round 1- Random. Let students communicate with each other without addressing what style of leadership or decision making they should use.

Round 2- Authoritarian style. Have the student outside the VR headset orchestrate the commands and decisions.

Round 3- Two-way democratic decision making. In this style, there is more back and forth communication between the participant inside the headset and the users who have access to the map.

Groups should play the game, taking turns after each bomb, for approximately 30 minutes.

Post-Application Guidelines & Reflections

Once the student/user has explored and navigated through the VR experience, they should answer the following questions:

- In which situation or round did you feel the communication and decision making was most effective in achieving your goal? Why?
- Which situation (round) was the least effective? Why?
- Was there ever a moment when you had trouble communicating clearly with others? What happened? How did you resolve the conflict?

- Have a look at this video, which talks about how VR can help improve decision-making while under stress, https://www.youtube.com/watch?v=ANLOysHPDOw. What do they hope to learn from the VR study?
- This VR experience is supposed to simulate what it might be like working as a spy team. What are some limitations to this experience that prevent it from being close to the real thing?

Extension Activities
- Other VR applications allow users to practice their communication skills. Try playing the game, Keep Talking and Nobody Explodes to enhance communication skills.
- Watch this documentary from Discovery Channel about air traffic controllers, Discovery - Understanding air traffic controllers, https://www.youtube.com/watch?v=u0nYEmrq1as. Write a report about why this profession is considered one of the most stressful in the world.

Lesson Guide: Effective Two-Way Communication
Keep Talking and Nobody Explodes VR
Designed by Craig Frehlich B.Ed., M.Ed.

© 2019 Springboard Virtual Reality, Inc.

Target Age:	Target Subject/Field:	Essential Idea:
10- Adult, Grade 5 and up	Interdisciplinary, Advisor/ Communication Skills	How can students communicate effectively to exchange thoughts, messages and information?

Goal of the Learning Application:

Effective two-way communication is paramount to understanding. Humans use a variety of different verbal and non-verbal cues to ensure that listeners can receive our message effectively. However, just like any skills, this requires explicit practice. In this VR application, we push our communication skills to the limit. In Keep Talking and Nobody Explodes, a player is tasked with disarming procedurally generated bombs with the assistance of other players who are reading a manual containing instructions. To defuse the bomb, the manual experts instruct the VR player on how to interact with the bomb while the VR player communicates details about the bomb to the manual expert. Time is of the essence as there is a countdown timer on each bomb, therefore being clear and concise regarding directions will enable your team to perform admirably.

Possible Learning Objectives:	Key Concepts & Vocabulary:
<ul><li>Students will be able to learn how to give and receive meaningful feedback effectively.</li><li>Students will be able to Interpret and use modes of non-verbal communication effectively.</li><li>Students will be able to read and interpret the text for comprehension.</li><li>Students will be able to read critically for comprehension.</li><li>Students will be able to develop strategies to improve communication within a group.</li></ul>	<ul><li>Non-verbal communication</li><li>Verbal communication</li><li>Effective communication</li></ul>

Pre-Application Guidelines & Questions:

Before entering the VR application, users should answer the following questions.
- Since VR can provide such a real and visceral experience, it will be essential to discuss and highlight that no one should try this if they feel any stress or anxiety related to the context of bombs or bomb defusal. Students should participate based on a volunteer-only model. Have an open discussion with students that the intent of this learning activity is not to celebrate the use of bombs.
- Watch this video clip about performing communication under pressure, https://www.youtube.com/results?search_query=bomb+diffusing+in+24. Why is it sometimes better to diffuse a bomb with more than one person?
- Watch this clip, https://www.youtube.com/watch?v=AZ0fmcgOjjo. Why is it important to conduct training exercises like this one for bomb defusal experts?
- Communicating during a stressful situation like an emergency might be different than regular day-to-day casual conversation. List some differences between these two situations.
- 911 dispatchers need to be trained to communicate in stressful situations. Have a look at this video, https://www.youtube.com/watch?v=IBwGcDO_FGg. What is one strategy you noticed that was helpful for the 911 dispatched to communicate?

Important Tips & Tricks to Consider Inside this VR Application

What to expect? When a student puts on the headset, they are placed inside a room with a chair and desk. On the wall is a poster showing students how the controller works to grab and click on things. To get started, the student will need to pick up the blue binder, and it will turn the page to a table of contents. If this is the first time for users, then clicking on "THE FIRST BOMB" is recommended. Once the first bomb is selected, the room goes dark, and a bomb will show up on the desk. The student should pick up the bomb and begin the game. Alternatively, students could click the black icon on the desk that says, "FREE PLAY."

Allow students to take turns, in groups of 3-5 people, using the VR headset to dismantle the bomb. The user can go into settings to adjust the timer on the bomb (5 min is the default). The participants will have to download and print off the bomb manual here, http://www.bombmanual.com/print/KeepTalkingAndNobodyExplodes-BombDefusalManual-v1.pdf.

Groups should play the game, taking turns after each bomb, for approximately 30 minutes.

Post-Application Guidelines & Reflections

Once the student/user has explored and navigated through the VR experience, they should answer the following questions:

- Which aspect or component of the bomb was the easiest to diffuse? Why?
- Which part or component of the bomb was the most difficult to diffuse? Why?
- Like a 911 dispatcher, asking yes/no questions can be an effective and efficient way to

- communicate in this game. To what extent were you and your group able to use yes/no type questions?
- When more than one team member is helping interpret that manual, it can get confusing regarding who is in charge. How did your group overcome this obstacle? What other strategies could you use besides the one that was adopted by your group?
- Non-verbal communication is usually an essential part of interacting with someone face to face. When you are talking on the phone, through email, or in this game, and you don't have the benefit of non-verbal communication, what should you consider to make communicating as effective as possible?
- As the time gets closer and closer to zero, we tend to get more stressed. What strategies did you adopt to minimize the stress when the counter got closer to zero?

Extension Activities

- Have students watch the documentary Bomb Doctors: The Men With Nine Lives, which can be found here, https://www.youtube.com/watch?v=Qba8c41ZfCk. Write a report about what it is like to be in this kind of profession or career.
- This game also has a computer version. Try playing it on the computer instead of in VR. With the computer version, non-verbal communication is possible. To what extent was the game easier or harder with the help of non-verbal communication?

Appendix B

VR Lesson Guides for Art Education

Appendix B

Lesson Guide: VR as a Tool to Preserve Culture
Masterpiece VR
Designed by Craig Frehlich B.Ed., M.Ed.

© 2019 Springboard Virtual Reality, Inc.

Target Age:	Target Subject/Field:	Essential Idea:
11+, Grade 6 and up	Art, Humanities, Social Studies	To what extent can VR be used as a tool to preserve cultural artefacts and therefore retain a culture's identity?

Goal of the Learning Application:

Conflict, weathering and modernization are all processes which may act as agents of change and prevent a culture from keeping important artefacts which represent the identity and historic fabric of a group of people. For example, during World War II, the Nazis stole and destroyed several monuments, pieces of art and other artefacts. How can we preserve these important pieces of cultural history? The application Masterpiece VR is an immersive tool that lets the user paint in 3D space with virtual reality. Should we use immersive VR programs like Masterpiece VR to recreate a digital representation of these artefacts to actively safeguard cultural identity?

Possible Learning Objectives:	Key Concepts & Vocabulary:
<ul><li>Students will be able to create novel solutions to complex problems.</li><li>Students will be able to analyse and evaluate an issue or idea.</li><li>Students will be able to use alternative forms of media to create and design a digital representation</li><li>Student will be able to visualize and design in 3D space.</li></ul>	<ul><li>Identity</li><li>Preservation</li><li>Culture</li><li>Interpretation</li><li>Representation</li></ul>

Pre-Application Guidelines & Questions:

Allow students access to the following news article and have them read it individually or as a class, https://calgaryherald.com/news/local-news/calgary-made-virtual-reality-game-teaches-blackfoot-language-culture.

Ask students to individually reflect on the following questions after reading the newspaper article:

Appendix B

- What is one thing the article made you think about?
- What is one thing the article made you wonder about?
- Do you think this was an effective way of preserving Blackfoot language and culture? Explain why or why not.

About the use of Masterpiece VR

Drawing and sculpting in 3D space requires some practice. Have students watch a few tutorials on how to sculpt in Masterpiece VR located here, https://www.youtube.com/watch?v=tHnwjkuqilQ and https://www.youtube.com/watch?v=Da27x64roQQ. And, give them some practice and discover time before getting them to start this assignment.

Important Tips & Tricks to Consider Inside this VR Application

Preserving Cultural Artefacts

An assignment for students to get a sense for how effective Masterpiece VR might be for preserving cultural artefacts and therefore the identity of a group of people might be the following.

The Canadian Government has hired you, the expert artist, to recreate an iconic and important piece of Canadian history and identity. The Thunderbird totem pole of the North Wester aborigine people of Vancouver Canada. Using the tools in Tilt Brush, the government has asked that your virtual reality piece be as real and authentic to the exact model as possible. Specifications and details of your real artefact are listed below. When you are done your piece take a screen capture in Masterpiece VR and includes images of your finished piece from several angles.

Here is a link to a creative commons image of a totem pole students might recreate in Masterpiece VR, https://pxhere.com/en/photo/183346. Students will need to be given details on Height, length etc.

Post-Application Guidelines & Reflections

Once the student/user has explored and navigated through the VR experience and recreated their totem pole they should answer the following questions:

- What are some positive aspects of using Masterpiece VR to recreate a totem pole?
- What are some limitations to using Masterpiece VR to create a totem pole?
- Give examples of some cultural artefacts that would be difficult to recreate in Masterpiece VR? Why?
- Replication of art and other artefacts is a very controversial subject. Original paintings can be powerful representations of the vision of the designer, however replicas can be "lost in translation". By making a copy or representation of something are we losing the ethos or intention? Explain.
- In a broader sense, do you think artists and designers should be commissioned to archive/ recreate important cultural artefacts for societies around the world? Why or why not?

Extension Activities

- Watch the (2013) movie "Monuments of Men" to see the struggle of trying to preserve Jewish cultural artefacts during WWII. Here is the trailer, https://www.youtube.com/watch?v=CreneTs7sGs. Write an essay outlining why it was important for this movie to be made.
- Read this article https://www.vice.com/en_us/article/nzea5q/how-an-inuit-filmmaker-is-using-virtual-reality-to-tell-her-cultures-stories and compare and contrast to the one that was read in the pre-application guidelines and questions.

Appendix B

Lesson Guide: Interrogating Scale, Space and Place
Sculptr VR
Designed by Craig Frehlich B.Ed., M.Ed.

© 2019 Springboard Virtual Reality, Inc.

Target Age:	Target Subject/Field:	Essential Idea:
10-adult, Grade 5 and up	Art, Design, Architecture/Prototyping	Transforming 2-D drawings into 3-D shapes can help us understand more about the impact an idea has on a space.

Goal of the Learning Application:
Designers can help transform spaces. In design and architecture, spaces can be used to create a stronger emotional response to an area. However, two-dimensional representations are not as powerful as seeing a 3-D model in VR. Sculptr VR makes it easy to create and explore brilliant new sculptures in virtual reality. Taking concepts in our heads and making them come alive in a virtual environment is quick and easy with Sculptr VR.

Possible Learning Objectives:	Key Concepts & Vocabulary:
<ul><li>Students will be able to visualize and design objects in a 3-D environment.</li><li>Students will be able to use and apply technology effectively as a means to model and create solutions.</li><li>Students will be able to develop an appreciation of the impact of design innovations for life, global society and environments.</li><li>Students will be able to use alternative forms of media to create and design a digital representation.</li></ul>	<ul><li>Scale</li><li>Space</li><li>Place</li><li>Living walls</li><li>Sustainability</li><li>Community</li><li>Transformation</li></ul>

Pre-Application Guidelines & Questions:
Before entering the VR application, users should answer the following questions.
- Designers are challenged with taking big ideas or concepts and transforming them onto paper and then into a 3-D prototype. Have a look at this video about this process, https://www.youtube.com/watch?time_continue=2&v=DVdmwz-mBxg&feature=emb_logo. How does the designer use VR as a tool to help him create a hotdog stand?

Appendix B 57

- Have a look at this VR design application, https://www.youtube.com/watch?v=hhn00WdjrCY, what are the benefits of using VR to design in a space?
- Spaces or environments can be transformed with the right installation. One type of installation that can make a space more serene and promote sustainability is the inclusion of Living Walls. Have a look at this news clip on living walls, https://www.youtube.com/watch?v=CcAAeGpLN4c. Besides reducing air pollution, what are some other benefits of living walls?
- Find a space in your school or building that would benefit from having a living wall. Research various types of living walls on the internet. Sketch out on an A4 piece of paper two possible living walls.
- Get feedback from various friends, classmates and other people who experience the space to see which living wall would be best to design in 3-D space. Which design idea will you make and why?
- Watch this 28 min video on how to use the essential tools of Sculptr VR, https://www.youtube.com/watch?v=Q0dHB_l66Ao.

Important Tips & Tricks to Consider Inside this VR Application

What to expect?

- Import your chosen 2-D sketch into Sculptr VR. To do this, scan the image you sketched onto your computer and then drag the image file into the folder called Sculptr VR images.

- Now enter the application and click on the icon on your pallet that looks like scenery. You should be able to see your image in there. Click on your image and scale its size. Using blocks and other shapes, re-create a 3-D version of your living wall. Be sure to make it as close to its original size as possible. Take a picture of your final product.

Post-Application Guidelines & Reflections

Once the student/user has explored and navigated through the VR experience, they should answer the following questions:

- Did your living wall turn out as you expected? Why or why not?
- Which part of your living wall was the hardest to recreate?
- Is drawing in 3-D easier or more difficult than drawing in 2-D? Why or why not?
- What are some aspects or things about your living wall that you noticed needed changing after you visualized it in 3-D space?
- What are some limitations to this 3-D sculpting program?
- How could it be improved?

Extension Activities
- Virtual Reality is a new medium. Have a look at this video, https://www.youtube.com/watch?v=hPNQv8FoxZs. Write a report discussing whether VR reality creations should be considered art?
- There are other applications in the SpringboardVR marketplace that allow you to create and design things. Try some of these VR applications: Masterpiece VR and ABC Paint VR.

Appendix B

Lesson Guide: Can VR Archive History?
The Kremer Collection
Designed by Craig Frehlich B.Ed., M.Ed.

© 2019 Springboard Virtual Reality, Inc.

Target Age:	Target Subject/Field:	Essential Idea:
10-Adult, Grade 5 and up	Arts, History/ Cultural Preservation	Can VR be used to preserve cultural identity and provide a window into history?

Goal of the Learning Application:
Archiving history is an essential endeavour in many societies. Having artefacts that give us clues to how we lived and shaped our heritage is a worthy intellectual endeavour. Culture and its heritage reflect and shape values, beliefs, and aspirations. Many believe that the past influences our future, but if there is no past, then it becomes difficult to forge a future. Physical museums and galleries provided venues to ensure cultural heritage and identify are achieved and preserved. Moreover, digital storage has played a significant role in the preservation of cultural heritage. It has enabled the sharing of cultural and historical heritage around the world. Digital storage is not only the most popular method of preservation, but it is the trend for the future. Can VR be an acceptable trend toward preserving our past? In this VR experience, the user will walk around a fantastic new space, where the balance between traditional museums and VR is represented through a new sort of architecture. The user is challenged to critique this experience and decide whether VR museums can act as an acceptable substitute for communicating our cultural heritage.

Possible Learning Objectives:	Key Concepts & Vocabulary:
• Students will be able to relate to the expressive and communicative potential of three-dimensional and/or digital media. • Students will be able to visualize in 3D space. • Students will be able to develop a familiarity with other cultural perspectives, which is essential to success in our globalized world. • Students will be able to evaluate alternative forms of media. • Students will be able to analyze and evaluate an issue or idea.	• Historical Evolution • Preservation • Diversity • Communication • Cultural Identity • Archives

Appendix B

Pre-Application Guidelines & Questions:
Before entering the VR application, users should answer the following questions.
- Have a look at this video clip, https://www.youtube.com/watch?v=aBO3iY_IJ8Y. Why do you think cultural heritage sites are sometimes destroyed during conflicts?
- Besides physical monuments, what are some other parts of culture that could be destroyed and forgotten if they are not preserved in some way?
- Watch this video, https://www.youtube.com/watch?v=35bbI38AMh4. Explain how technology is acting to preserve many heritage sites around the world.
- There is an inherent danger to transforming history from one form to another. We have to trust the process of transformation will be accurate. The worry is that it might be "lost in translation." Find an example in history when something was transformed for preservation and inaccurately portrayed.
- What are some ways that technology might mistranslate a form of history from one medium to another?
- Imagine a situation whereby you can look at a painting in real life and then look at its recreation on a computer. How might they be different? How might they be the same?

Important Tips & Tricks to Consider Inside this VR Application

What to expect? Allow the user to browse around the museum for approximately 15 minutes.

Users should look at examples of paintings from a variety of different artists. As they browse the collections, they should make a note of the style of each painter and be able to synthesize characteristics that make up the identity of the painter from looking at their work. Additionally, users should become aware of what story the paintings are trying to say about the culture and ways of life of the Dutch people in the 17th century.

Post-Application Guidelines & Reflections

Once the student/user has explored and navigated through the VR experience, they should answer the following questions:

- These paintings represented life in the 17th century. Describe what culture was like, as depicted in the pictures.
- Peter Lastman was Rembrandt's teacher and had a painting in this collection called "The Parable of the Good Samaritan." Additionally, there is another painting of Christ with his hands bound over his head. Why did many painters pick biblical topics to paint about during this period?
- Lighting has been optimized for this VR collection through the special photogrammetry. In a physical museum, how do curators ensure optimal lighting?
- What were some benefits of looking at artistic works in VR? What were some drawbacks?
- The paintings in this museum are of different sizes. Why is this the case?
- Pick two paintings that were memorable for you. What were they about, and why were they so significant?

- Do you feel there was anything "lost in translation"? Explain
- Curators of virtual museums will need to have standards regarding their collections. What sorts of criteria should be adopted when establishing a VR museum?

Extension Activities
- Several artists are experimenting with the medium of VR to create art. Have a look at this video, https://www.youtube.com/watch?v=hPNQv8FoxZs. Why are many artists gravitating to this new way of creating art?
- SpringboardVR has several applications on its portal that allow users to create virtual works of art. Try one of these VR experiences to create artwork in this new medium: Masterpiece VR, Sculptr VR, and ABC Paint VR.

Appendix C

VR Lesson Guides for Problem Solving and Puzzles

Appendix C

Lesson Guide: The Key to Problem Solving
A Fisherman's Tale
Designed by Craig Frehlich B.Ed., M.Ed.

© 2019 Springboard Virtual Reality, Inc.

Target Age:	Target Subject/Field:	Essential Idea:
10-Adult, Grade 5 and up	STEM, Interdisciplinary/Problem Solving	Flexible thinking is the key to successful problem solving by establishing new frameworks and considering alternative connections to objects, processes and systems.

Goal of the Learning Application:

Solving complex problems can sometimes be frustrating. One often has to see new connections to unfamiliar situations. Teaching problem solving is never easy as it goes beyond memorizing and requires users to reframe situations to come up with new pathways. Being able to look at a problem from a different point of view is one strategy used by successful problem solvers. One has to question their assumptions and alter their ways of thinking. Furthermore, sometimes finding these new pathways are entrenched in our cultural biases. With practice, users can often overcome obstacles that are paramount to problem-solving and make connections resulting in success. In this learning experience, users will practice flexible thinking to solve a VR puzzle game. In a Fisherman's Tale, users are challenged to bend the laws of physics to help Bob, a tiny fisherman puppet, overcome a storm to reach the top of a lighthouse.

Possible Learning Objectives:	Key Concepts & Vocabulary:
• Students will be able to use flexible thinking to make unexpected connections to solve a problem. • Students will be able to consider multiple alternatives, including those that might be unlikely or impossible to solve a problem. • Students will be able to reflect on and consider cultural bias to solve a problem. • Students will be able to apply skills and knowledge in unfamiliar situations.	• Systems • Perspective • Strategy • Flexible Thinking • Cultural Norms • Reframing ideas • Scale

Appendix C 63

Pre-Application Guidelines & Questions:

Before users enter the VR applications have them reflect by answering the following questions;
- Solving riddles is a form of problem-solving. Have users consider the following riddles;
    - A magician promises that he can throw a ball as hard as he can and have it stop, change direction, and come back to him. He claims he can do it without the ball bouncing off of anything, the ball being tied to anything or the use of magnets. How is this possible? The Answer is here-https://www.riddles.com/u/riddle/6718.
    - Sergi and Sally were sitting in their family room one night. While Sergi was watching tv, his wife Sally was reading. All of a sudden, the power went out, and Sergi decided to go to bed, but Sally kept on reading. With no use of artificial light, Sally kept on reading. How? The Answer is here- https://www.riddles.com/1080.
- Escape rooms are growing in popularity around the world. Watch this video about escape rooms, https://www.youtube.com/watch?v=zwgaTYOx0RI. What were the 10 tips given to succeed in escape rooms?
- When it comes to problem-solving, what is a "red herring"?
- Try this online escape room, http://neutralxe.net/esc/r1.html, and attempt to use the 10 tips given in the previous question.
- Which escape room tips seemed most useful?
- It is believed by many that our cultural bias might limit our ability to solve problems. For example, if we are familiar with an object, we might tend to use the traditional way. However, if someone has never seen the object before, they might think of novel ways to use the object. Find an example of when this might be true.

Important Tips & Tricks to Consider Inside this VR Application

What to expect?

The user will need to use flexible thinking to find connections between objects to solve puzzles and move through the story.

There is an exciting gameplay in A fisherman's Tale. The player has to switch between a tiny version of the game and the real-life version. So, when something is done in one version, it is also done in the other. By switching back and forth between the two perspectives, clues can be found and puzzles solved. Scale becomes a critical consideration in the gameplay. For example, the user can put an object in real life into the smaller version to make the object bigger. Allow the user to play the game for approximately 25 minutes.

Post-Application Guidelines & Reflections

Once the student/user has explored and navigated through the VR experience, they should answer the following questions:

- What were some of the easiest puzzles you encountered in this VR experience?
- What were some of the hardest puzzles you encountered in this VR experience?

- Did you encounter any "red herrings"? Give an example of one from A Fisherman's Tale.
- Give an example of when you were "stuck" at a particular puzzle. What did you do to overcome this impasse?
- List some tips or strategies you used in this VR application from what you learnt about solving escape rooms.
- How is problem-solving in this VR application similar and different from solving problems in escape rooms?
- Were there any puzzles that might be difficult to solve because of cultural bias? Explain.
- How can users overcome cultural bias in problem-solving?

Extension Activities

- Users can design their own escape room. Go to https://www.breakoutedu.com/. Follow the website directions and links to find out how you might create your private escape room.
- Several other VR applications focus on problem-solving. Here is a list of other highly immersive VR applications that will enhance your problem solving and flexible thinking skills: The Gallery-Call of Starseed, I Expect You to Die, and Free Diver Down.

Lesson Guide: Elastic Thinking Improves Problem-Solving
The Gallery: Call of the Starseed
Designed by Craig Frehlich B.Ed., M.Ed.

© 2019 Springboard Virtual Reality, Inc.

Special Note: Many ideas for this lesson guide came from author, Leonard Mlodinow, and his book "Elastic Thinking."

Target Age:	Target Subject/Field:	Essential Idea:
12-Adult, Grade 7 and up	Science, Psychology/Problem Solving	Elastic thinking can unlock our problem-solving skills and enable us to solve complex situations with high speed and ease.

Goal of the Learning Application:
"Where there is a will there is a way". This saying relates to one's resilience and grit to overcome obstacles. When we engage in problem-solving, we often require large doses of grit, resilience and patience. Nevertheless, being astute at problem-solving can also be taught. Our brain often switches between rigid analytical thinking needed for logic and nimble elastic (divergent) thinking required to solve complex problems. Psychological research has shown that we can train our brains to be more flexible in our thinking and get better at solving agile, complex problems. In this VR experience, you will discover what effect strategies like mindfulness and positivity have on improving our divergent/elastic thinking abilities.

Possible Learning Objectives:	Key Concepts & Vocabulary:
• Students will be able to create novel solutions to complex problems. • Students will be able to practice flexible thinking to solve problems. • Students will be able to make connections to groups of unfamiliar things and transfer that new knowledge to agile problems. • Students will be able to practice observing carefully in order to think divergently. • Students will be able to revise and reframe understanding based on new information and evidence. • Students will be able to analyze complex concepts into their constituent parts and synthesize them to create new understanding.	• Mindfulness • Elastic Thinking • Divergent Thinking • Change • Problem Solving

Appendix C

Pre-Application Guidelines & Questions:

- The Nine-dot Problem is a classic problem. The goal of the puzzle is to link all 9 dots using four straight lines or fewer, without lifting the pen and without tracing the same line more than once. Try the Nine Dot Problem below,

https://presentmomentmindfulness.com/wp-content/uploads/2017/12/Nine-Dots-Puzzle-Present-Moment.pdf

You can find the answer to the Nine-dot Problem here,
https://en.wikipedia.org/wiki/Thinking_outside_the_box#/media/File:Ninedots.svg

- One strategy to help us unlock our potential to "think outside the box" and gain new insight into solving problems is tapping into our unconscious mind via mindfulness. Read this article, https://hbr.org/2019/01/how-mindfulness-can-help-engineers-solve-problems, and answer the following question. What were some of the strategies suggested listed in the article to evoke mindful thinking to improve one's problem-solving abilities?
- There appears to be a correlation between happiness and problem-solving. Have a look at this video on happiness, https://www.ted.com/talks/shawn_achor_the_happy_secret_to_better_work?language=en and answer the following questions;
    a. What is the message in the TED Talk?
    b. How does this apply to problem-solving?
    c. How can we improve our mood, which may enhance our problem-solving abilities?
- Word association games can sometimes flex our divergent thinking muscles and enhance our problem-solving by seeing new connections. Try this divergent thinking game, https://research.google.com/semantris/. Did your score improve as you continued the game? Why?
- How is divergent thinking related to elastic thinking?
- Watch this video, https://www.youtube.com/watch?v=-fOe9pPCW-c. What are some ways that you can get better at elastic thinking?

Important Tips & Tricks to Consider Inside this VR Application

What to expect? Allow the user to play this VR application for approximately 20 minutes.

When the user first enters the application, they are presented with an option to put various cassette tapes into a tape player, depending on what section of the game they want to play. Have users new to The Gallery put in the yellow cassette tape. As the user moves around the beach-like scene they must interact with various objects to find clues and connections. Items they collect of importance can be stored in the virtual backpack. The user will need to employ multiple elastic thinking strategies as they try and solve puzzles and advance through the game. For example, when they are stuck, they should adopt a mindfulness technique (i.e. take a break from teleporting around, breath deep and shut out distractions). Additionally, students could pause the experience to increase their level of happiness by watching a funny video and then enter the VR experience again. Employing these strategies are meant to increase elastic thinking and improve the user's ability to solve problems.

Post-Application Guidelines & Reflections

Once the student/user has explored and navigated through the VR experience, they should answer the following questions:

- Describe a clue or connection that you felt was easy in the first part of the puzzle game.
- Describe a clue or connection between objects that were particularly difficult to know or solve. In the end, how were you able to figure out this divergent connection?
- When you were stuck on trying to solve a problem in The Gallery, what kind of mindfulness strategy did you use to help you calm the mind and unlock elastic thinking? Was it successful in helping you move forward in the game?
- The flare gun becomes an essential tool in this part of the puzzle game. What clues did the game reveal that led you to know that the flare gun was critical in moving the puzzle game forward?
- Unlocking the power of our brain is not new. People have been trying to tap into the hidden potential of the mind for years. One strategy is electrical stimulation. Have a look at this video, https://www.youtube.com/watch?v=Iu0H0csxLmM. Would you be willing to use trans-cranial electrical stimulation to try and enhance your brain's abilities? Why or why not?

Extension Activities

- Watch the blockbuster movie, A Beautiful Mind (the trailer can be found here, https://www.youtube.com/watch?v=WFJgUm7iOKw). Write a report on what made John Nash, one of the most brilliant minds of his time.
- To practice your problem-solving skills, get access to the physical game Mindtrap, which can be found here, https://www.amazon.com/Mind-Trap-Brain-Teaser-Board/dp/B008KS31O6, and find some people to play it with.

Appendix C

Lesson Guide: Form and Function in Virtual Reality
Fantastic Contraption

Designed by Craig Frehlich B.Ed., M.Ed.

© 2019 Springboard Virtual Reality, Inc.

Beginner Content-Note this guide is intended for players new to this application. Additional guides will be available for intermediate and advanced levels

Target Age:	Target Subject/Field:	Essential Idea:
10-Adult, Grade 5 and up	Science, Engineering/Physics	Machines can be adapted to improve mobility and stability and function to meet human needs.

Goal of the Learning Application:
Players must build a device or "contraption" that is both mobile and capable of transporting a jelly ball object from point A to B. The mobile contraption will optimally operate like a tank, rolling over obstacles and knocking down blockades. Players can choose from 5 different objects when building their contraption. There are 3 wheels: one that spins clockwise, one that spins counter-clockwise, and one that will not rotate until pushed or moved by momentum. There are also two connectors: a solid stick and a water stick. The water stick can pass through walls and wheels, but not everything. Players have free reign when designing their contraption, so trial and error plays a major role in this learning experience. But what makes a structure strong, stable and rigid in order for it to complete its task?

Possible Learning Objectives:	Key Concepts & Vocabulary:
<ul><li>Students will be able to infer how the stability of a model structure will be affected by changes in the distribution of mass within the structure and by changes in the design of its foundation and parts.</li><li>Students will be able to create novel solutions to complex problems.</li><li>Students will be able to identify points in a structure where flexible or fixed joints are required, and evaluate the appropriateness of different types of joints for the particular application.</li><li>Students will be able to apply scientific skills and knowledge in unfamiliar situations.</li><li>Students will be able to combine scientific knowledge, understanding and skills to create products or solutions.</li></ul>	<ul><li>Adaptation</li><li>Form</li><li>Function</li><li>Stability</li><li>Moveable Joint</li><li>Rigid Joint</li></ul>

Pre-Application Guidelines & Questions:

Before entering the game/application here are some ways to engage students in ideas to prepare them for success.

Consider The Importance of Shape in your Design.
- Design a square out of 4 strips of cardboard (each approximately 8cm long) and stick pins in them so then hold together.
- Stand the square up and apply a force to it downwards. What happens?
- Now apply a force horizontally. What happens?

Now design a triangle shape out of 3 of the strips of cardboard.

- Stand the triangle upward and apply a force to it downwards on the top, What happens?
- Now apply a force horizontally? What happens?
- Have a look at this video, https://www.youtube.com/watch?v=r-2UIZU8u0M, what did you learn?
- Find some pictures of structures that utilize triangular shapes to keep them strong and insert them into this document or draw them by hand below.
- What is the difference between a fixed and movable joint?

Important Tips & Tricks to Consider Inside this VR Application

What to expect?

When players first enter the game they are introduced to how the game works and the controls. For example, they first learn how to change the size of a stick (an important building block) as well as how to join them together. Additionally, players also learn how wheels work to propel structures forward. Users are given shadows to guide them on how to build their first contraption before they enter real game play. The tutorial takes approximately 3-5 minutes. When the user finishes their first contraption they are presented with Neko, a cat, that holds all the materials/parts the user will need to build your next contraption. The user should start building their second contraption. In the interest of time, allow the user to build and advance levels for approximately 20 minutes before they move on to the post game questions.

Post-Application Guidelines & Reflections

Once the student/user has explored and navigated through the VR experience they should answer the following questions:

- Sketch one or two of your Fantastic contraption designs. In the space provided below. Label all your parts.
- Engineers and designers always use trial and error when designing structures. Sometimes your first ideas are not successful. Explain how you used trial and error in designing one of your contraptions.
- The key idea for Fantastic Contraption is that machines can be adapted to improve mobility and stability and function to meet human needs. Let's say you were an engineer who was hired by a firefighting company to design a vehicle that extinguished fires on the third floor of a building. Using only materials like those used in Fantastic Contraption, design and draw a prototype of what your device might look like.

Extension Activities

- The music band, Ok Go, using contraptions in their music videos. Have a look at this TED Talk on how designers of these experiences have learnt a lot about building and problem solving, https://www.youtube.com/watch?v=uarlIjkHlAs . Please note, between the time (5:17-5:22), there is an offensive word, so you might need to fast forward that part. What is one thing you agreed with from watching this Ted talk. What is one thing you disagreed with? What is one thing you learnt from watching this Ted talk.
- Try this engineering type building game online to enhance your building and problem solving skills even further, http://www.engineering.com/gamespuzzles/dynamicsystems.aspx.

Appendix D

VR Lesson Guides for STEM Education

Lesson Guide: Simple Machines Make Our Lives Easier
Gadgeteer VR
Designed by Craig Frehlich B.Ed., M.Ed.

© 2019 Springboard Virtual Reality, Inc.

Target Age:	Target Subject/Field:	Essential Idea:
9-adult, Grade 4 and up	Science, STEM, Design, Engineering/ Simple Machines	Simple machines can manage the transfer of energy in complex devices to make our lives easier.

Goal of the Learning Application:
Complex machines play a big part in our world. Buildings, roadways, and playgrounds are examples of complex infrastructures that utilize the understanding of simple machines. Aristotle once said, "The whole is greater than the sum of its parts." When individual parts are connected to form a complex machine, they are worth more than if the pieces were in isolation. Simple machines help transfer energy to reduce the effort it takes for us to do work. And, when combined into a complex machine, they can allow us to innovate. *Gadgeteer* is a physics-based VR puzzle game that tasks users with building machines to solve complex puzzles with a wide variety of parts.

Possible Learning Objectives:	Key Concepts & Vocabulary:
<ul><li>Students will be able to identify six basic types of simple machines.</li><li>Students will be able to predict and explain the results in the object's change of motion in a complex system.</li><li>Students will be able to develop a model to generate data for iterative testing and modification of a proposed object, tool, or process such that an optimal design can be achieved.</li><li>Students will be able to practice observing to recognize problems.</li><li>Students will be able to practice analyzing and attributing causes for failure to come up with a solution.</li><li>Students will be able to predict and evaluate the movement of an object by examining the forces applied to it.</li></ul>	<ul><li>Work</li><li>Efficiency</li><li>Interactions</li><li>Systems</li><li>Movement</li><li>Levers</li><li>Fulcrum</li><li>Torque</li></ul>

Appendix D

Pre-Application Guidelines & Questions:
Before entering the VR application, users should answer the following questions.
- Have a look at this basic video on simple machines, https://www.youtube.com/watch?v=P7xS2Ali1t8. What are the different types of simple machines?
- Have a look at this video, https://www.youtube.com/watch?v=qybUFnY7Y8w. List and identify as many simple machines as you can from the video.
- Watch this video, https://www.youtube.com/watch?v=8hrFBYp5LYs. What is a mechanical advantage? Why is it helpful to increase the mechanical advantage in a simple machine?
- Watch this video, https://www.youtube.com/watch?v=yngNoWnwomw. Why do many roadways incorporate the screw, which is a twisting incline plane, into their design and infrastructure?
- Try this online interactive simple machine site, http://www.cosi.org/downloads/activities/simplemachines/sm3.html. What was the most challenging part of the online interactive?

Important Tips & Tricks to Consider Inside this VR Application

What to expect? Allow the participant to design and build for approximately 20 minutes.

When you first enter this VR application, you will be presented with a tutorial on how to grab, manipulate, copy/clone and reset objects in the application. The tutorial takes about 5 minutes.

Once the tutorial is over, the user will need to go to the Sandbox section. Here you will have a library of objects to build your complex machine. Be sure to include at least four simple machines into your contraption.

Post-Application Guidelines & Reflections

Once the student/user has explored and navigated through the VR experience, they should answer the following questions:

- Sketch your final complex machine and list the various types of simple machines located in your contraption.
- Which simple machines were the most difficult to incorporate into your complex machine? Why?
- Which simple machines were easiest to incorporate into your complex machine? Why?
- In this physics simulation, friction was kept to a minimum. How was this accomplished? Why is it essential to keep friction to a minimum when designing complex machines?
- Give an example of when increasing friction would be advantageous when designing simple or complex machines?
- Combining simple machines to create a useful invention is often tricky as there are so many moving parts that need to work together as a team. Try this interactive simulation to practice combining elements to make a whole, http://sciencenetlinks.com/interactives/powerplay.html.

Extension Activities
- Try this engineering-type building game online to enhance your building and problem-solving skills even further, http://www.engineering.com/gamespuzzles/dynamicsystems.aspx.
- Rube Goldberg was an American cartoonist and engineer who drew complex elaborate contraptions that allowed humans to complete simple tasks. His inventions were poking fun at how the idea or principle that machines should be designed to be as simple as possible when completing a function or task. Click on the example;

  "Self-Operating Napkin – Rube Goldberg." https://www.rubegoldberg.com/artwork/self-operating-napkin/. Accessed 3 Sep. 2019.

  Write a report about Rube Goldberg and why his ideas were an essential contribution to society.

Appendix D

Lesson Guide: Heart Physiology and Gender
Sharecare VR

Designed by Craig Frehlich B.Ed., M.Ed.

© 2019 Springboard Virtual Reality, Inc.

Target Age: 13-adult, Grade 8 and up	Target Subject/Field: Science, Biology/ Heart Physiology	Essential Idea: What are the implications of physiological gender differences in the human heart?

Goal of the Learning Application:
From anatomical and physiological perspectives, males and females differ. In this learning application, you will look at the human heart to visualize how it looks in immersive 3D space. You will be able to control the rate of the heartbeat and make predictions on how this might affect males and females in their daily lives. Sharecare VR is a real-time simulation of the human body. Sharecare VR allows anyone to freely navigate and explore an anatomically accurate 3D model of the human body, its organs, and its natural function. Visualize how the body works. Explore organs and systems in a fully immersive 3D.

Possible Learning Objectives:	Key Concepts & Vocabulary:
• Students will be able to describe the overall size, location and function of a human heart. • Students will be able to compare and visualize how a human male heart differs from a female heart. • Students will describe and visualize how an average male heartbeat differences from a female heartbeat rate. • Students will be able to compare difference electrocardiographs of males and females	• Diversity • Causation • Adaptations • Systems • Electrocardiograph • Heart Valves

Pre-Application Guidelines & Questions:
Before entering the VR application, users should answer the following questions. • Have a look at this video on the structure and function of the heart. https://www.khanacademy.org/science/health-and-medicine/circulatory-system/circulatory-system-introduction/v/meet-the-heart. What is the primary purpose of the heart? The heart is a muscle; how does it get oxygen? • Have a look at this video on how blood flows through the heart. https://www.khanacademy.org/science/health-and-medicine/circulatory-

system/circulatory-system-introduction/v/flow-through-the-heart. The left ventricle has a lot more muscle tissue around it than the right ventricle, why is this the case?
- Have a look at this article comparing some anatomical gender differences, https://gendermed.org/just-the-facts/. How is the structure and function of the male heart different than women?

Important Tips & Tricks to Consider Inside this VR Application

What to expect? The user should spend approximately 10-15 minutes in the VR application.

When you enter this VR application, you are given a tutorial on how the controls work.

Once the user has understood the controls, they should select the male gender and then a healthy heart. Turn the labels on and look at the various parts. Then, select the heartbeat and move the slide to 70 beats per minute. Now click on the ECG button to expose the electrocardiograph. Take a picture of what you see using the picture tool. Now click on the heart symbol to take you inside the heart to see how the valves and muscles operate.

Use the back arrow to go to the main screen and change the gender to female. Click on the menu to pull up the female heart with the labels exposed. Change the heart rate to 80 beats per minute. Now click on the ECG button to reveal the electrocardiograph. Take a picture of what you see using the picture tool. Now click on the heart symbol to take you inside the heart to see how the valves and muscles operate.

Post-Application Guidelines & Reflections

Once the student/user has explored and navigated through the VR experience, they should answer the following questions:

- What were the benefits of viewing the various parts to the heart in immersive VR?
- What is an ECG? How do the images of the ECG differ between males and females? Why?
- Why do you think, on average, females have a higher heart rate than males?
- As it relates to the structures inside the heart (i.e. valves that open and close), do you think it is an advantage or disadvantage to have a faster heart rate? Explain
- Is it an advantage or disadvantage to have a higher heart rate as it relates to sports? Explain.
- Some believe women are catching up to men when it comes to performance in athletics. Have a look at this video clip, https://www.youtube.com/watch?v=HWm1MyCPhZs. Do you think this is true? Explain.
- Besides the heart and sex organs, what other organs differ between males and females?
- How do you think these differences impact their daily lives?

Extension Activities

- Artificial hearts can be used as a substitute for a real human heart. Have a look at this video, https://www.youtube.com/watch?v=Gv9xB9HQsww. What are the advantages and disadvantages of artificial hearts?
- Try this online virtual heart simulation. https://www.abc.net.au/science/lcs/heart.htm. Why is heart surgery sometimes considered a high-risk operation?

Lesson Guide: Using VR to Connect with Nature
Fujii VR

Designed by Craig Frehlich B.Ed., M.Ed.

© 2019 Springboard Virtual Reality, Inc.

Target Age:	Target Subject/Field:	Essential Idea:
11-Adult, Grade 6 and up	Science, Biology/Ecology	To what extent can VR be used to foster a greater connection and appreciation toward nature?

Goal of the Learning Application:

Our relationship and connection with nature, especially plants, is faint despite our dependence on them for food and clean air. This feeble connection may be due to a lack of respect for plants. Humans see themselves as superior organisms because we have brains and are perceived to be more intelligent. Can we use immersive VR to strengthen our relationship with plant?. Advocates of virtual reality claim that VR creates embodied experiences which are so real that our brain makes strong empathetic and emotional connections. In this VR application, you will act as a caretaker for nature, especially plants. In Fujii, the land of Fujii has been abandoned, left to fall into darkness and dormancy. It's the player's duty to explore, grow, and help revive nature back to health. Watering, touching, and interacting with plants and creatures throughout each biome will help restore their life force and expand the ring of light in the sky above.

Possible Learning Objectives:	Key Concepts & Vocabulary:
<ul><li>Students will be able to learn to practice empathy towards nature.</li><li>Students will be able to explain the balance of energy and matter exchange in nature and explain how this maintains equilibrium.</li><li>Students will develop an understanding of how human activities can disrupt the balance and equilibrium between humans and nature.</li><li>Students will be able to revise understanding based on new information and evidence.</li></ul>	<ul><li>Systems</li><li>Connection</li><li>Balance</li><li>Relationships</li><li>Consequences</li><li>Anthropomorphism</li></ul>

Pre-Application Guidelines & Questions:

Plants may be smarter than we think and deserve more respect. Listen to this episode of the podcast Radiolab, https://www.youtube.com/watch?v=_w7MHmebvrM. Answer the following questions;
- In the podcast episode, how did the plants learn to wrap their roots around water pipes underground?

- Describe the experiment that the scientist did on the Mimosa plant to demonstrate that they can learn.
- Were the Radiolab hosts able to repeat the experiment? Explain.
- Describe the Pavlov-type experiment that Monica did on the pea plants. What did it prove?
- Would you respect and revere plants more if you knew they were able to learn? Explain.
- What is anthropomorphism?
- What were some of the critiques and complaints about Monica's experiments on plants?
- To what extent do you think humans would do more to protect nature if they knew that nature was more human-like?

Important Tips & Tricks to Consider Inside this VR Application

What to expect?

When users enter Fujii, they are given a short tutorial on how to move around, grab objects, and navigate through biomes (nature scenes). Additionally, the tutorial demonstrates to the user how to plant and water a seed and how to unlock doors or portals into new biomes. The tutorial takes approximately 3 minutes. The basics of the gameplay is to use water and other resources to collect objects like seeds to unlock portals to new areas or biomes. Allow the user to engage and experience Fuji for approximately 20 minutes.

Post-Application Guidelines & Reflections

Once the student/user has explored and navigated through the VR experience, they should answer the following questions:

- When you first enter Fujii, the game developer tries to enhance the user's embodied experience by giving them arms and hands. Describe what that felt like.
- What were some of your favorite parts of this VR application?
- As a caretaker of nature in this VR application, what were some of your chores or responsibilities?
- How did the player bring balance or equilibrium to each nature area (biome)?
- How are plants and animals interdependent of each other?
- Were there any examples of anthropomorphism in this VR application? Explain. Did this help you care for nature more?
- With our help, we can enhance the quality of each nature area (biome) and bring it back to life, creating a balance with nature. List some ways we might be better caretakers in the real world to create a more sustainable future with nature.
- How did this VR application enhance our understanding that we are interdependent with plants?
- After playing Fujii, do you feel more reverence and empathy toward nature? Why or why not?

Extension Activities

- Repeat the Mimosa drop experiment to see if the plant can learn from its experiences. Be careful to ensure that plants are not damaged or harmed during your experimental design and execution.
- Deforestation continues to plague our ecosystems and disrupt the balance and equilibrium we have with the earth. Watch this video clip, https://www.youtube.com/watch?v=2yMnMJWyY7k . Write a persuasive essay on why we need to do more to stop deforestation.

Appendix D

Lesson Guide: How Can We Stop Pollution?
Oceans We Make

Designed by Craig Frehlich B.Ed., M.Ed.

© 2019 Springboard Virtual Reality, Inc.

Target Age:	Target Subject/Field:	Essential Idea:
10-Adult, Grade 5 and up	Ecology, Science/Oceanography, Sustainability	Immersive VR may evoke empathy and instil greater compassion for environmental issues.

Goal of the Learning Application:
Users will play the role of a diver who is immersed in a beautiful ocean only to find that it has been polluted with garbage. Using stunning visuals and straightforward gameplay, this underwater experience will leave you thinking about our beautiful oceans and what we can do to save them - all in under 5 minutes. Can immersive VR help convince you to take action?

Possible Learning Objectives:	Key Concepts & Vocabulary:
• Students will be able to investigate and describe relationships between humans and their environments. • Students will be able to analyze personal and public decisions that involve consideration of environmental impacts and identify needs for scientific knowledge that can inform those decisions. • Students will be able to identify examples of human impacts on ecosystems and investigate and analyze the link between these impacts and the social wants and needs that give rise to them.	• Empathy • Change • Environmental Stewardship • Sustainability • Interdependence

Pre-Application Guidelines & Questions:
Have users watch this video, https://www.youtube.com/watch?v=WfGMYdalClU, and answer these questions.
- List some environmental concerns found in the video.
- What message is the video trying to portray?
- Why do you think some people mistreat the earth?
- What percentage of the earth is made of ocean?
- Why are oceans important to our earth?
- The earth is a delicate system. Many living things rely on each other to survive. Give an example of an organism that lives in the ocean that humans rely on for survival.

Important Tips & Tricks to Consider Inside this VR Application

What to expect?

This short VR experience invites the user to take a 4-minute journey scuba diving through the ocean. Along the way they discover shocking truths about how we are treating our planet.

Post-Application Guidelines & Reflections

Once the student/user has explored and navigated through the VR experience, they should answer the following questions:

- What was the most common type of waste you encountered in the ocean journey?
- Have a look at this video, https://www.youtube.com/watch?v=CEpkkogDCdY, what have been some positive results of the ban? What have been some negative?
- Enforcing a ban is one way to keep garbage out of the ocean. What are some other strategies we could adopt to keep our oceans clean?
- Some chemists have developed biodegradable plastic. Have a look at this video, https://www.youtube.com/watch?v=REYgK58kuSY. What was surprising about the video?
- Oceans are one of our largest ecosystems. They are filled with complex feeding relationships called food webs. Give an example of how garbage might affect a food web.
- Watch this video on empathy, https://www.youtube.com/watch?v=-0r0q6WMfo8. What is empathy? What are some reasons why we should be more empathetic to oceans and their situation?
- There are many ways to raise awareness of critical environmental issues like ocean pollution. To what extent does VR make a person more empathetic toward this issue?
- Besides pollution, what are some other issues we need to worry about related to oceans?

Extension Activities

- Have a look at this Ted Talk, https://www.youtube.com/watch?v=P8GCjrDWWUM. Design a campaign at your school, town or city to raise awareness about plastic bag pollution.
- Sharks are essential animals in our oceans. However, many fishermen are killing sharks at an alarming rate. Watch the full documentary Sharkwater (you can watch the trailer here-https://www.youtube.com/watch?v=RQYHBrtYsnk) and write a report or make a presentation about why shark finning needs to be banned.

Appendix D

Lesson Guide: Who Is the Smartest?

Lifeliqe VR Museum

Designed by Craig Frehlich B.Ed., M.Ed.

© 2019 Springboard Virtual Reality, Inc.

Target Age: 11-Adult, Grade 7 and up	Target Subject/Field: Science, Biology/Brain Science	Essential Idea: To what extent does the size of the brain affect an organism's intelligence?
Goal of the Learning Application: Is bigger always better? Being taller does not always mean faster. What about the brain? Do organisms with bigger brains have a higher level of intelligence? In this learning experience, you will use the VR application Lifeliqe to investigate the brains of various animals and predict whether brain size is linked to animal intelligence. Lifeliqe VR Museum allows students to understand complex science concepts by providing immersive 3-d content that can be seen from multiple points of view and scaled to various sizes.		
Possible Learning Objectives: • Students will be able to investigate and interpret diversity among species. • Students will be able to analyze how brain size relates to thinking and intelligence. • Students will be able to predict whether intelligence changes over time in various organisms? • Students will be able to compare, contrast and draw connections from new forms of media and technology.		**Key Concepts & Vocabulary:** • Evolution • Development • Biological Diversity • Adaptation • Intelligence

Pre-Application Guidelines & Questions:
Some animals are smarter than others. Many can demonstrate emotions and solve problems. Have a look at this example, https://www.youtube.com/watch?v=2s2RNK0Bmp8.
• Why would many think that the raccoon in the video is smart?
• What do you think influences how smart an organism is?
• What are mammals? Research how mammals think differently than other organisms.
• Look up how many neurons are present in the brains of the following:
    o Ants
    o Whales
    o Dolphins
• What was surprising about your answers to question 4?		

Important Tips & Tricks to Consider Inside this VR Application

What to expect?

Firstly, participants are asked to observe a short tutorial on how to move around, size and scale objects. Then, users should view the "Animal Biology" tab and expand this menu by clicking on the three dots to the far right, which are labelled "show more." This will allow students to look at the anatomy of several organisms. More specifically, students should observe the size of their brains. The user should pick the following organisms: dog anatomy, horse anatomy, great white shark anatomy, perch anatomy, and red-eared slider anatomy (turtle).

Post-Application Guidelines & Reflections

Once the student/user has explored and navigated through the VR experience, they should answer the following questions:

- Order the organisms you viewed in VR from those that had the smallest brain to those that had the largest brain.
- From your observation of brain size, do you think intelligence is a result of the size of an organism's brain? Explain
- Watch this video, https://www.youtube.com/watch?v=D5yyBHLL34s. How has this influenced your thinking about whether the size of an organism's brain affects its intelligence?
- Ants have limited brain capacity and think differently than many other organisms. Ants are like automatons and are programmed to think in fundamental terms. A colony of ants exhibit a collective brain. Ants portray mindless automated thinking, yet as a group they can process collectively and be able to problem-solve. Do you think humans are capable of this kind of thinking? Justify your answer.
- The evolutionary process helps organisms evolve. Is intelligence governed by evolutionary processes? That is to say, do organisms develop larger brains over time?

Extension Activities

- Solving problems is considered a form of higher-order thinking. With the rise of AI (artificial intelligence), humans are worried that computers will surpass them in thought. Watch this TED talk on the subject, https://www.youtube.com/watch?v=MnT1xgZgkpk. Write a report or design a presentation on what your opinion is about the topic. Do you think computers will ever surpass human intelligence?
- Besides our brains, pick another piece of animal anatomy and discuss whether having a larger size of this part would be advantageous or not?

Appendix D

Lesson Guide: VR as a Tool for Embodiment

Richie's Plank Experience

Designed by Craig Frehlich B.Ed., M.Ed.

© 2019 Springboard Virtual Reality, Inc.

Target Age: 12+, Grade 7 and up	**Target Subject/Field:** Science, Biology, Psychology/Human physiology	**Essential Idea:** The human cognitive brain can be tricked into believing an experience or situation is real with the right technology.

Goal of the Learning Application:
Advocates for virtual reality claim that it is one of the only mediums that can accomplish embodiment whereby the user perceives themselves inside the body of another user sometimes called an "Avatar". In this experience the user truly believes they are in another person's shoes so to speak. Their emotions and physiological behaviours are based on the actions of the avatar within the virtual reality world. In this education application we will put this claim to the test. Does virtual reality accomplish full human embodiment? One part of Richie's Plank Experience allows the user to enter a virtual elevator that will take them to the top of a high rise building. The doors open at the top and the user is able to walk out on a plank suspended 80 floors above a busy city. The user will use a heart rate monitor to act as a measure of increased fear or anxiety. There is also an opportunity to add spiders to the plank for additional emotional response. Furthermore, a physical plank can be customized and calibrated to increase the realism of the experience.

Possible Learning Objectives:	**Key Concepts & Vocabulary:**
• Students will be able to draw reasonable conclusions and generalizations. • Students will be able to challenge themselves to overcome fears. • Students will be able to make guesses and generate testable hypotheses. • Students will be able to identify trends and forecast possibilities. • Students will be able to use models and simulations to explore complex systems and issues. • Students will be able to investigate and describe the	• Embodiment • Environment • Perception • Interaction • Physiology • Psychology

Appendix D

factors that affect the healthy function of the human systems. • Students will be able to describe changes in body functions in response to changing conditions.	

Pre-Application Guidelines & Questions:

Have students watch this video or show it on a large screen for the entire class to watch, https://www.youtube.com/watch?v=vl_B6nz3UOQ

Ask students to individually reflect on the following questions:

- What are some of the most common fears people experience? Why?
- If fear is our most primal emotion, can we control it? Explain.
- Why do some people crave fear?
- What are some ways that fear manifests itself in our body?
- Can we manipulate fear through VR experiences? Explain.

Important Tips & Tricks to Consider Inside this VR Application

What to expect? *Disclaimer. If users have a severe fear of heights then it is advised for them to proceed with caution. It may be wise to remind students that they may remove the headset at any time and the experience will go away.* The VR experience takes approximately 5 minutes to go up the elevator onto the floor with the plank. It may take some time for the student to walk out onto the plank depending on how scared they are of heights in virtual reality.

Explain to students that they will be asked to put on a VR headset, take a ride in a virtual elevator to the top of a skyscraper and be asked to walk on a plank 80 stories above a city.

Get students to design a hypothesis for what they believe will happen to their heart rate when exposed to extreme heights in virtual reality by answering the question below.

- How will your heart rate be affected by being exposed to extreme heights in virtual reality? Why?

Instructions- Once the students have designed their hypothesis, they are ready to experience Richie's Plank Experience with a device on their wrist that monitors heart rate (ie. a garmin or apple watch). When the heart rate monitoring device has been set up and started, allow the student to enter the elevator and go to the top 80th floor. When the elevator door opens invite students to look down on the city and walk along to plank slowly and come back. Get them to enter the elevator again and take it back to the bottom floor. Stop the heart rate monitor system on the watch and collect the data and complete the table below.

Time in Seconds	Instantaneous Heart Rate (Beats/minute)

Get students to graph their results.

Pool class data to together and analyse trends in class data.

Step 2- Repeat this experiment by adding a real wooden plank on the ground. Obtain a real wood plank and follow the procedures in the application to calibrate the plank on the floor. See this video for help, https://www.youtube.com/watch?v=7IHawkLhYog

Results with real wooden plank

Time in Seconds	Instantaneous Heart Rate (Beats/minute)

Get students to graph their results.

Pool class data to together and analyse trends in class data.

Post-Application Guidelines & Reflections

Once the student/user has explored and navigated through the VR experience they should answer the following questions:

- What was your conclusion to this experiment?
- Were results as you expected? Explain why or why not.
- Was there a difference in results when a real wooden plank was included in the application? Why or why not?
- List some aspects/elements of this experiment that would affect the accuracy/realism of your results and conclusions.
- In your opinion, does virtual reality cause full embodiment? Explain.

Extension Activities

- Repeat this experiment several times to the same subject to see if people with prolonged exposure to the plank are able to lower their heart rate over a period of time. Reflect on whether VR could be used to cure people of a fear of heights.
- Repeat this experiment by adding spiders to the end of the plank and analyse and reflect on results.
- Immersive VR is being used to try and cure war veterans with post-traumatic stress disorder (PTSD) through exposure therapy. Watch this video, https://www.youtube.com/watch?v=VA6FEXLN5KA, and discuss one thing you agreed with and one thing you disagreed with from this video.

Appendix D

Lesson Guide: Is Diet Related to Survival?

Feed a Titanosaur VR

Designed by Craig Frehlich B.Ed., M.Ed.

© 2019 Springboard Virtual Reality, Inc.

Target Age:	Target Subject/Field:	Essential Idea:
10-adult, Grade 5 and up	Science, Geography, History/Dinosaurs	Can an organism's eating habits help determine its survival?

Goal of the Learning Application:
There are several theories on what caused the Dinosaurs to die out or become extinct. One is that their food source ran out. In this VR application, you will see a giant herbivore dinosaur up close and get an opportunity to experience what it is like to feed it. Come face to face with one of the largest creatures to ever walk the planet Earth and feed it! The object of this bite-sized educational project is to allow amazing facts to be delivered in an immersive VR experience, with a focus on our Titanosaur – Argentinosaurus.

Possible Learning Objectives:	Key Concepts & Vocabulary:
• Students will be able to understand what type of food a Titanosaur eats. • Students will be able to predict and infer how eating habits influence an organism's survival. • Students will critically analyze various reasons why dinosaurs became extinct.	• Diet • Behaviour • Adaptation • Change • Extinction

Pre-Application Guidelines & Questions:
Before entering the VR application, users should answer the following questions.
- Have a look at this video, https://www.youtube.com/watch?v=Up2nggJkqNk. Why is the Titanosaur famous? List some essential facts about the Titanosaur.
- There are several theories on what killed the dinosaurs. Have a look at this video, https://www.youtube.com/watch?v=JqGphEaJvDE. According to the video, what is the main reason why all the dinosaurs died out? What proof do they have?
- Some organisms are plant eaters (herbivores), like the Titanosaur. List some large herbivores that are alive today on the earth. Why do you think many herbivores are so large?
- What is an Argentinosaurus? How did it get the name?
- If organisms are not able to adapt to a changing environment, they die out and become extinct. Mass extinction is rare but can occur. Have a look at this video, https://www.youtube.com/watch?v=36b9ox8iF24. What caused the extinction of the Dodo birds?

Important Tips & Tricks to Consider Inside this VR Application

What to expect? This VR application lasts approximately 15 minutes.

The user enters the environment and has to feed the dinosaur branches from a tree. Then, they are invited to teleport around the dinosaur to get a sense of size and scale.

Post-Application Guidelines & Reflections

Once the student/user has explored and navigated through the VR experience, they should answer the following questions:

- Give an estimate as to how much taller the Titanosaur is than a human.
- Besides the branches of a tree, what do you think are some other types of food that the Titanosaur eats.
- From looking inside its mouth, what parts make it clear that it must be a plant-eater?
- Have a look at this video, https://www.youtube.com/watch?v=JqGphEaJvDE. What are some reasons why many of the herbivore-type dinosaurs are so large?
- Would the Titanosaur still be alive today if it was able to adapt to eating meat? Explain.

Extension Activities

- Watch the documentary, "The Day the Dinosaurs Died," you can find the trailer here, https://www.youtube.com/watch?v=soqPEswKaDo. Write a persuasive paper outlining which theory is most plausible on how the dinosaurs became extinct.
- Check out this video on the T-Rex in VR, https://www.youtube.com/watch?time_continue=3&v=cxaibw-ei7M&feature=emb_logo. What are the benefits of learning about dinosaurs in VR?

Appendix D

Lesson Guide: Controlling the Flow of Energy
Short Circuit VR

Designed by Craig Frehlich B.Ed., M.Ed.

© 2019 Springboard Virtual Reality, Inc.

Target Age:	Target Subject/Field:	Essential Idea:
13-adult, Grade 8 and up	Science, Physics/Electricity	We have a responsibility to monitor and control energy systems that are used to improve the quality of our lives.

Goal of the Learning Application:
Energy is a powerful and highly useful part of our lives. It allows us to adapt, innovate and live a high quality of life. Electricity, heat and moving water are just a few examples of the types of energy we harness to make our lives better. But, with power comes responsibility. Understanding and being able to monitor and control energy is essential to our safety and survival. In this VR application users will investigate how electrical energy is harnessed and controlled. Short Circuit VR is an electronics lab simulator in Virtual Reality. You can build your own electronic circuits with the components provided and learn basic electronics by completing challenges.

Possible Learning Objectives:	Key Concepts & Vocabulary:
<ul><li>Students will be able to assess the potential danger of electrical devices, by referring to the voltage and current rating (amperage) of the devices; and distinguish between safe and unsafe activities.</li><li>Students will be able to use switches and resistors to control electrical flow and predict the effects of these and other devices in given applications.</li><li>Students will be able to measure voltages and amperages in circuits.</li><li>Students will be able to apply Ohm's law to calculate resistance, voltage and current in simple circuits.</li><li>Students will be able to develop, test and troubleshoot circuit designs for a variety of specific purposes.</li></ul>	<ul><li>Energy</li><li>Control</li><li>Systems</li><li>Circuits</li><li>Resistance</li><li>Voltage</li><li>Ohm's Law</li><li>Current</li><li>Open Circuit</li><li>Closed Circuit</li><li>Electrical Breadboard</li></ul>

Pre-Application Guidelines & Questions:
Before entering the VR application, users should answer the following questions.
- Have a look at this video, https://www.youtube.com/watch?v=VnnpLaKsqGU. What is the difference between an open and closed circuit?
- This VR application is called Short Circuit. Watch this video, https://www.youtube.com/watch?v=zorqwY2a8gI. Why are short circuits dangerous?
- In this application you will use an energy source (battery), a conductor (wire), a load (LED lights) and sometimes a control (switch). Electrical breadboards are used to design your circuits. Have a look at this video to understand how to use breadboards, https://www.youtube.com/watch?v=6WReFkfrUIk. Why is it important to understand how the layout of the breadboard works for electrical circuits?
- Setting up a closed-circuit whereby energy flows from one area to another to light up a bulb is useful for humans. However, the amount of energy (voltage of battery) and how fast the current is flowing needs to be controlled and monitored. If we push the electrons with a strong battery this can be dangerous and may generate excess harm. It is possible to slow down the current in a closed circuit to ensure we are not doing any damage or harm by using resistors. We often use a mathematical formula called Ohm's law to help us determine how much voltage, current and resistance is needed. Have a look at this video to understand more about Ohm's Law, https://www.youtube.com/watch?v=F_vLWkkOETI. If the voltage is increased in a circuit, what happens to current? If resistance is increased in a circuit what happens to current?
- Try these Ohm's Law questions http://ohmlaw.com/ohms-law-quiz-with-answers/ and see if you can get the correct answers.

Important Tips & Tricks to Consider Inside this VR Application

What to expect? Allow the user to design two basic circuits within the application which should take approximately 20 minutes.

When the user enters this VR application, they are presented with several challenges related to creating electrical circuits using a breadboard, batteries, wires and various other controls and loads. There is a whiteboard that provides instructions on theory and supports their understanding of how to design the various challenges. Ultimately, the user should be able to complete the following:

- Design a circuit that lights up an LED bulb (this will require a resistor and the use of Ohm's law to figure out how big or small of a resistor is needed)
- Design a circuit that lights up an LED bulb with a switch.

Post-Application Guidelines & Reflections

Once the student/user has explored and navigated through the VR experience, they should answer the following questions:

- Were you successful the first time you designed your circuit with the battery, wires and LED bulb? Why are why not?
- Why does the 1.5 Volt battery not work to light up the LED bulb?

Appendix D

- Why is a resistor needed in order to design a circuit with a 9v battery and an LED bulb?
- From your calculation of Ohm's law, what size of resistor was needed to light up the LED bulb?
- What was the most challenging part of adding a button or switch to the second circuit on the breadboard?
- We learnt in the pre-application that short circuits can be dangerous. The breadboard helps us map out the flow of electricity for our circuits but in real life, we don't often use breadboards. What other electrical safety devices are used to prevent circuits from overloading and being unsafe?
- This learning guide focused on understanding and controlling electricity. Have a look at this video, https://www.youtube.com/watch?v=amLtmYw7GuM. Research and find out how this can be prevented.

Extension Activities

- Students can design, discover and learn more about interactive electrical circuits here, https://phet.colorado.edu/en/simulation/legacy/battery-resistor-circuit.
- This application provides opportunities to explore other aspects of electrical circuits. Investigate how some of these other electrical components work in an electrical circuit and play with them in this investigation: diodes, photoresistors, and/or potentiometers.

Lesson Guide: Adapting to the Changing Environment
VR Regatta
Designed by Craig Frehlich B.Ed., M.Ed.

© 2019 Springboard Virtual Reality, Inc.

Target Age: 10-Adult, Grade 5 and up	Target Subject/Field: Physical Education, STEM/ Sailing, Basic Physics	Essential Idea: Adapting to a changing environment can enhance our experience in sport.

Goal of the Learning Application:
Some sports rely heavily on understanding the conditions of the environment. Wind, waves, changes in elevation are all factors that might affect our performance in some sports. Knowing how to harness these changing conditions is paramount. Sailing is a sport that requires that you leverage the wind for movement. Adjusting the sail to the changing wind conditions involves knowledge and skill. In this VR application, the user will learn how to refine their sailing skills by controlling the mainsail and the direction of the boat. Reading the prevailing conditions and adapting to an ever-changing environment will enhance the users' success.

Possible Learning Objectives:	Key Concepts & Vocabulary:
• Students will be able to understand how a sail works to provide forward movement and propulsion in the water. • Students will be able to adjust the mainsail for different wind conditions in order to move the boat forward at varying speeds. • Students will be able to do simple navigation, moving North, South, East, West, recognizing landmarks, and navigating around buoys.	• Adaptation • Change • Forces • Mainsail • Tiller • Mainsheet • Rudder

Pre-Application Guidelines & Questions:
Before entering the VR application, users should answer the following questions.
- Understanding the forces that affect how a sailboat moves in the water is essential. Have a look at this video, https://www.youtube.com/watch?v=M4CQ4T_K8Hw. Why is having a tailwind (wind coming from the back) not the most optimum situation?
- Using the video in the previous question, in which situation do the boat and wind have to be for the boat to go the fastest?
- Have a look at this page on the wind on a sail, https://www.nauticed.org/freesailingcourse-m1-33. What happens when you move the slider in the animation to the far right? Why does this slow the boat down?

Appendix D

- Flapping sails is not suitable for the optimum speed. Have a look at this video, https://www.youtube.com/watch?v=viL-3f9MYJw. How do we minimize this phenomenon?
- Besides wind flow, what other types of changing forces do we need to consider and adapt to while sailing?
- Navigating while sailing requires some skill and practice when working with the rudder. Have a look at this video, https://www.youtube.com/watch?v=25ILEDlMyjQ. What is one of the most important things to keep in mind while steering the boat with a rudder?

Important Tips & Tricks to Consider Inside this VR Application

What to expect? Allow the user to spend approximately 20 minutes in this VR application.

Tutorial-When the user first enters the VR application, they are invited to try the tutorial to practice sailing. While sailing in the tutorial, the user will have control over the direction of the mainsail using the mainsheet. Additionally, the user must also steer the boat with the tiller, which is connected to the rudder. In the tutorial, it will be essential to try and adjust the mainsail to maximize your speed related to the wind direction, while at the same time use the tiller to control the course of the boat. The tutorial should take approximately 5-8 minutes, depending on how well you keep your speed up. Try and maintain a speed above 2.

First Race- Inside the building, the user will have to teleport to a different room to access the races section. While in the race section, the user should pick the "easy race" first. After that, the user should select additional races to hone and refine their skills.

Post-Application Guidelines & Reflections

Once the student/user has explored and navigated through the VR experience, they should answer the following questions:

- What was your time for your first race? What was your maximum speed?
- Describe the position of the mainsail compared to the wind during the time your boat was travelling the slowest and fastest.
- Body positioning and feeling comfortable in the boat is essential. Describe what your optimal body position was for sailing.
- What was the direction of the wind for your first race? How often did the wind change during your first race? What did you do to adapt or adjust?
- After the first race, what were some things to pay closer attention to before entering the second race?
- What was your time on the second race? Did you improve? Why or why not?
- What sailing skills did you feel you were doing better at in your second race? Explain.
- This VR application is very realistic; however, it is not perfect. What are some of the limitations to this application compared to real-life sailing?

Extension Activities

- Try this free boating game, https://www.youtube.com/watch?v=zlsW_zQYvQI. What are some similarities and differences between operating a catamaran and a sailboat?
- The sport of sailing is evolving. It will have new categories for the 2024 Olympics. Have a look at this article, https://edition.cnn.com/2018/05/15/sport/sailing-olympics-2024-new-events-spt/index.html. What is your opinion regarding this new change to the sport of sailing? Is it fair?

Appendix D

Lesson Guide: Catapults and Levers
Fantastic Contraption
Designed by Craig Frehlich B.Ed., M.Ed.

*Intermediate Content-Note this guide is intended for players who have had some previous experience and have advanced beyond the first few levels of this application.

© 2019 Springboard Virtual Reality, Inc.

Target Age: 10-adult, Grade 5 and up	Target Subject/Field: Science/Physics, Engineering, Problem Solving.	Essential Idea: Understanding energy transfer can improve our efficiency of machines.

Goal of the Learning Application:
This lesson guide assumes that players already have some familiarity with Fantastic Contraption and are looking to advance their skills and understanding. Players must build a device or "contraption" that is capable of transporting a jelly ball object from point A to B. Players have free reign when designing their contraption, so trial and error plays a significant role in this learning experience. Using rigid sticks to build a stable structure with triangles has already been explored in a previous lesson guide. This lesson guide will focus on how to use the transfer of energy associated with levers and catapults to do work. Devices or Contraptions should be stationary and fling the jelly ball toward its target.

Possible Learning Objectives:	Key Concepts & Vocabulary:
• Students will understand various classes of levers. • Students will be able to build or modify a model mechanical system to provide for different force ratios (input force vs output force). • Students will be able to evaluate the design and function of a mechanical device in relation to its efficiency and effectiveness and identify its impacts on humans and the environment. • Students will be able to investigate and describe the transmission of force and energy between parts of a mechanical system. • Students will be able to infer how the stability of a model structure will be affected by changes in the distribution of mass within the structure and by changes in the design of its foundation and parts.	• Energy Transfer • Levers • Fulcrum • Adaptation • Resources • Form • Function • Forces

Pre-Application Guidelines & Questions:

Before entering the VR application, users should answer the following questions.
- Have a look at these two videos on levers, https://www.youtube.com/watch?v=YlYEi0PgG1g and https://www.brainpop.com/technology/simplemachines/levers/. What do we have to do to our force arm of a lever to lift more massive objects?
- Have a look at this video on different types of levers, https://www.youtube.com/watch?v=J2Nt_rRa3JY. Which lever is the most inefficient?
- What is torque? How could it be used as a force in levers? Provide examples or pictures from the internet of levers that use torque as a force.
- Catapults were used in ancient times to launch objects. Have a look at this video clip on catapults, https://www.youtube.com/watch?v=egZhg7v4NRs. What was the common name for these types of levers?
- Watch this basic video on how Fantastic Contraption works in VR, https://www.youtube.com/watch?v=nx-esx_KbJE&feature=emb_logo. Now sketch out on paper what your lever-type fantastic contraption might look like.

Important Tips & Tricks to Consider Inside this VR Application

What to expect? Allow the user to build and advance levels for approximately 20 minutes.

The user should already have some experience with Fantastic Contraption. Please see the beginner lesson guide for a basic understanding. One hint that may not have been part of the beginner lesson guide is the use of "sticky jelly," which is located on the underside of the cat. This can provide greater rigidity to joints.

Advance the levels to level 7, "Welcome to Small Gap Island."

Players can choose from 5 different objects when building their contraption. There are two wheels to consider: one that spins clockwise, one that rotates counterclockwise. In this level, sticks can be attached to the centre of the spinning wheel to provide a force. There are also two connectors: a solid stick and a water stick. The water stick can pass through walls and wheels, but not everything.

The objective for "Small Gap Island" should be to design a catapult or lever-type device that throws or flings the jelly ball to the jelly wall.

Post-Application Guidelines & Reflections

Once the student/user has explored and navigated through the VR experience, they should answer the following questions:

- Were you successful in designing a lever-type contraption that could fling the jelly ball to the target? Why or why not?
- What was one of the most challenging parts of designing your lever-type contraption?
- Sketch your final lever-type contraption that was able to throw the jelly ball the farthest in the level "Small Gap Island." Label your sketch with items like (force/effort arm, load arm, fulcrum)

- What type of lever did you end up building (Class 1, Class 2 or Class 3)? Why?
- Describe some changes or modifications you made from the original sketch that you made in your pre-application questions. Why did you have to make these changes from your original design?
- What did you notice happened when you adjusted the length of the load arm in the application? Did it fling your jelly ball farther?

Extension Activities

- Try this catapult simulator, https://sigmazone.com/catapult/. What was your farthest throw? What factors did you need to throw the ball the farthest?
- Pumpkin Chunkin is a show hosted by the Discovery Channel. You can watch the trailer here, https://www.youtube.com/watch?v=7VrS5hhEgz0. Find an episode of Pumpkin Chunkin on the internet and watch these incredible machines in action. Which one was your favourite? Why?

Appendix D

Lesson Guide: Using VR to Understand the Scale of the Universe
Titans of Space Plus

Designed by Craig Frehlich B.Ed., M.Ed.

© 2019 Springboard Virtual Reality, Inc.

Target Age:	Target Subject/Field:	Essential Idea:
9+, Grade 4 and up	Science/Astronomy	Students will discover our relationship between humans and the distribution of matter through space with an emphasis on scale and space in the universe and the ramifications.

Goal of the Learning Application:
How big is big? Our modern understanding of space has developed in conjunction with advances in techniques for viewing distant objects through manned space exploration. The Universe is very, very big. But just how big it is and how we fit into the scale of space can be quite difficult for a person to grasp. The distances and sizes are so far beyond our everyday experience but with the help of this immersive VR experience, a person can get a better sense for how big and far objects are in space and dive deeper into understanding the consequences of this phenomenon.

Possible Learning Objectives:	Key Concepts & Vocabulary:
<ul><li>Students will be able to describe, in general terms, the distribution of matter in star systems.</li><li>Students will be able to identify evidence for, and describe characteristics of, bodies that make up the solar systems and stars; and compare their composition and characteristics with those of Earth.</li><li>Students will be able to recognize that the other eight known planets, which revolve around the Sun, have characteristics and surface conditions that are different from Earth; and identify examples of those differences.</li><li>Students will be able to understand that Earth, the Sun and the Moon are part of a solar system that occupies only a tiny part of the known universe.</li></ul>	<ul><li>Place and space</li><li>Systems</li><li>Relationships</li><li>Perspective</li><li>Inner planets</li><li>Outer planets</li><li>Star</li><li>Development</li></ul>

Pre-Application Guidelines & Questions:

Have students go to this site, https://scaleofuniverse.com/, and have them scroll or move the slider from small to big and then ask them the following questions,

- Why is it helpful to understand the scale of things in our solar system and beyond?
- Our universe is dynamic and in flux. For example, our earth is changing. Give an example of something that is changing in our universe?
- As bodies in the universe age and develop what will be important to consider?

Important Tips & Tricks to Consider Inside this VR Application

What to expect?

The participant enters a spaceship-like object and has control over a dashboard. They start out exploring our planets in the solar system (inner and outer planets) and then discover things about the various types of stars. The experience takes about 20 minutes. Be sure to see how the planet spins on its axis by using the left-hand controller to simulate this.

Post-Application Guidelines & Reflections

Once the student/user has explored and navigated through the VR experience they should answer the following questions:
- Why do the inner planets closer to the sun lack moons compared to the outer planets?
- Most planets spin on their axis, how does the spin of the inner planets compare to the outer planets? Why is this the case?
- Our sun is a young star, with a specific colour and size. After looking at various other stars in our universe, explain how size and colour relates to the age of a star.
- As our sun ages it will change. What are the ramifications for bodies in our solar system as our sun changes? Explain.
- Although this VR application has some very realistic aspects to it, what is one aspect that is not realistically accurate in this VR simulation?
- The size of our universe is still up for debate. Is it finite or infinite? What do you believe?

Extension Activities

- To interact and learn more about star temperature and colour try this simulation, https://phet.colorado.edu/sims/html/blackbody-spectrum/latest/blackbody-spectrum_en.html , the user can adjust the sliders on the right change various factors.
- Check out the VR application, Universal Sandbox. Play with some of the controls and pose inquiries and test them out.
- Have a look at this video on the expanding universe, https://www.universetoday.com/116229/whats-causing-the-universe-to-expand/ , what are the consequences of an expanding universe?

Lesson Guide: Adapting for Life on Land
Dissection Simulator: Frog Edition

Designed by Craig Frehlich B.Ed., M.Ed.

 springboard VR

© 2019 Springboard Virtual Reality, Inc.

Target Age:	Target Subject/Field:	Essential Idea:
12-Adult, Grade 7 and up	Science, Biology/Anatomy, Physiology	Animals can develop structures that will help them adapt and function in new environments.

Goal of the Learning Application:
Is animal dissection immoral and unethical or a worthy scientific exercise that will unlock new insights into anatomy and physiology? Many educators believe that there is no substitute for actually viewing the real structures on the frog and having the actual experience of dissection. Can immersive VR provide a viable alternative to physical dissection? In this VR experience, the user will learn about the anatomy and physiology of a frog and connect these ideas to how it has evolved to be adapted for land and water.

Possible Learning Objectives:	Key Concepts & Vocabulary:
• Students will be able to describe the appearance and function of various organs found in the frog. • Students will be able to describe how the appearance and function of various organs in the frog compare to that of a human. • Students will evaluate the ethical implications of using animals for dissection. • Students will be able to identify various organs and tissues that have contributed to a frog's adaptation to land and water. • Students will be able to use technology to solve a problem or gain a new perspective on an issue.	• Transformation • Form • Function • Ethics • Adaptation

Pre-Application Guidelines & Questions:
Before users enter the VR applications, have them reflect by answering the following questions after watching this video by PETA, https://www.youtube.com/watch?v=yDtRoFPw74I.
• What are some benefits and drawbacks of this video?
• Do you agree with PETA's stance on animal dissections? Explain.

- Is there ever a case when dissections are justified?
- Frogs are amphibians that live both on land and in water. Give some adaptations they have evolved to live in both environments.
- Frogs are cold-blooded, which means they need to be warmed up by their environment. How does this impact where they live?
- Frogs have some organs that humans do not. List two organs that exist in frogs but not humans.

Important Tips & Tricks to Consider Inside this VR Application

What to expect? This VR application takes approximately 20 minutes.

When the user enters the VR experience, they are presented with a tutorial on how to navigate the room and various tools and instruments. A virtual frog will be placed on the dissection table, and a teacher will walk the user through the VR dissection.

Post-Application Guidelines & Reflections

Once the student/user has explored and navigated through the VR experience, they should answer the following questions:

- When you look inside the mouth, what unusual features do you notice about the tongue?
- What is the largest organ in the body cavity, and what are its functions?
- What are some characteristics that enable the frog to live on land?
- How is the heart of the frog different than a human heart? Why?
- How do classroom frog dissections contribute to the study of human biology?
- What were some benefits of doing the frog dissection in the virtual world?
- What were some drawbacks to doing the frog dissection in the virtual world?

Extension Activities

- Besides immersive VR, there are other alternatives to real dissection on the internet. Have a look at this virtual frog dissection, http://www.mhhe.com/biosci/genbio/virtual_labs/BL_16/BL_16.html, and compare and contrast this experience to the immersive VR application.
- Have a look at this video about limestone frogs in the Philippines, https://www.youtube.com/watch?v=HQ7g0qq-4G4. What makes them specialized and different from other frogs? Find another frog on earth that has changed or evolved to specialize and write a report about its unique characteristics.

Appendix E

VR Lesson Guides for Storytelling and Narrative Education

Lesson Guide: The Efficacy of VR Legends
Crow: The Legend VR

Designed by Craig Frehlich B.Ed., M.Ed.

© 2019 Springboard Virtual Reality, Inc.

Target Age:	Target Subject/Field:	Essential Idea:
10-adult, Grade 5 and up	Language Arts, Social Studies/ Narratives, Native Legends	To what extent can immersive VR communicate an influential legend to teach people about cultural values?

Goal of the Learning Application:
Immersive VR is a powerful communication tool. How effective can it be at conveying a Native American Legend? Native Americans have been predominantly oral storytellers. They used narratives in the form of legends to pass down essential beliefs, customs and values, especially as it relates to nature and the land. Can the new medium of VR effectively pass-on cultural values? The story of the Rainbow Crow is a Lenape legend, focusing on the concepts of sacrifice and commitment. After a long period of cold weather, the animals of the community become worried. They decide to send a messenger to the Great Sky Spirit to ask for relief.

Possible Learning Objectives:	Key Concepts & Vocabulary:
<ul><li>Students will be able to reflect on new understanding and its value to self and others.</li><li>Students will be able to appreciate the effectiveness and artistry of print and nonprint narratives.</li><li>Students will understand and appreciate how Native American legends can be used to teach people about cultural values.</li><li>Students will be able to interpret, evaluate and effectively use different modes of communication from alternative media sources.</li></ul>	<ul><li>Commitment</li><li>Legend</li><li>Sacrifice</li><li>Selflessness</li><li>Service</li><li>Culture</li><li>Transformation</li></ul>

Pre-Application Guidelines & Questions:
Before entering the VR application, users should answer the following questions.
- What is a legend?
- Why do Native Americans rely on legends to preserve their cultural history?
- In Native American culture, animals and nature often act as symbols for human characteristics. Have a look at this video, https://www.youtube.com/watch?v=7fve66nkKy4. What did the wolf symbolize? Why?

- The Native American legend of the Rainbow Crow can be found here, https://americanfolklore.net/folklore/2010/09/rainbow_crow.html. What was the goal of the Rainbow Crow? Why was he considered selfless? What did he bring to the forest community? How did the crow transform physically and emotionally? What was the moral or message from the print-based legend?

Important Tips & Tricks to Consider Inside this VR Application

What to expect? This story lasts approximately 20 minutes.

- During parts of the narrative, the user may use their hand controllers to interact with the scenes.

Post-Application Guidelines & Reflections

Once the student/user has explored and navigated through the VR experience, they should answer the following questions:

- What was your favourite part of the VR version of this story?
- How was the VR version similar and different than the print version you read in the pre-application section.
- Which version do you think was most effective at communicating the meaning and message? Explain.
- Sometimes oral and print stories or legends are more powerful because they enable us to use our imagination. Do you think VR narratives rob us of this opportunity? Explain.
- What are the benefits and drawbacks of converting a culturally rich experience like telling oral legends into the VR narrative?
- Have a look at this article, https://www.opengovasia.com/virtual-reality-to-preserve-aboriginal-culture/. How is VR in this article helping to preserve culture? What are some other ways that VR could enhance traditional cultures like the Native Americans?

Extension Activities

- Besides VR experiences, games may also raise awareness, empathy and understanding toward cultural identity. Try this game to learn more about the people of Haiti, https://ayiti.globalkids.org/game/.
- Watch the legend of the Raven here, https://www.youtube.com/watch?v=hB3SgMP9QW8. Write a paper about the symbolism of the Raven and why it was necessary for the Native North American tribe, Haida.

Appendix E

Lesson Guide: VR as a Medium for Storytelling
Firebird La Peri

Designed by Craig Frehlich B.Ed., M.Ed.

© 2019 Springboard Virtual Reality, Inc.

Target Age:	Target Subject/Field:	Essential Idea:
9+, Grade 4 and up	Language Arts/Narrative	To what extent can storytelling be compelling when the author has limited control over the audience's perspective?

Goal of the Learning Application:

Perspective is the position from which we observe situations, objects, facts, ideas, and opinions. Different views may lead to multiple representations and interpretations. In virtual reality, the viewer is allowed to explore, look around, and gaze in numerous locations to establish a variety of perspectives. Unlike conventional video narratives, VR users have a higher degree of agency and freedom. Does this new ability enhance or diminish the audience's imperative (meaning and message of the story or narrative)? In Firebird La Peri, you will experience a story told with the immersive power of VR. What does it look like? How will it feel? Can the author effectively create meaning and connect you to the tale?

Possible Learning Objectives:	Key Concepts & Vocabulary:
• Students will be able to appreciate the effectiveness and artistry of print and nonprint narratives. • Students will be able to interpret, evaluate, and effectively use different modes of communication from alternative media sources. • Students will be able to experiment with a variety of strategies, activities, and resources to explore ideas, observations, opinions, experiences, and emotions.	• Perspective • Audience imperatives • Point of view • Freedom of expression • Agency

Pre-Application Guidelines & Questions:

Have students watch individually or as a whole class the 360 video (keep in mind that the video allows the viewer to scroll around the scenes), The Pearl, https://www.youtube.com/watch?v=WqCH4DNQBUA. Invite students to reflect on this experience by answering the following questions;

- In what ways does this story, The Pearl, differ from a traditional video?
- What intended message(s) do you think the author was trying to convey in this story?

- To what extent is controlling the perspective critical in telling a story?
- Was having the agency (the ability) to scroll around the car and scene helpful in helping your understanding of the story in The Pear? Why or Why not?

Important Tips & Tricks to Consider Inside this VR Application

What to expect? This interactive Virtual ballet takes approximately 15 minutes.

When the person enters the VR experience, they are presented with a book that helps provide a narrative story about a dancer. *La Péri* is based on the music of on a one-act ballet of the same name by French composer Paul Dukas and tells the story of Iskender, an aging Magi who seeks the Flower of Immortality for La Peri. There are interactive elements as well as the use of light and sound to enhance presence within the narrative. For example, at one point, the listener has to catch a monkey-like creature and manipulate objects.

Post-Application Guidelines & Reflections

Once the student/user has explored and navigated through the VR experience, they should answer the following questions:
- At the end of this experience, the viewer has a choice between giving the dancer immortality or eternal grace, which did you pick and why?
- What do you think would happen if the VR user picked the opposite scenario?
- What was the moral or message to the story of the dancer in Firebird La Peri?
- In what ways does this story or narrative differ from a traditional video?
- How does this VR experience compare to watching the 360-degree video, The Pearl?
- In Firebird La Peri, the author tries to use strategies and techniques to control the perspective of the viewer who has a lot of agency to look around. What are some of these strategies?
- Is storytelling in immersive VR more or less compelling than traditional video? Justify and explain your position.

Extension Activities
- Watch this TED talk about storytelling in VR, https://www.youtube.com/watch?v=TOtTIWBrtJI. And write about something you agreed with and something you disagreed with.
- Research the original ballet, https://en.wikipedia.org/wiki/La_P%C3%A9ri_(Dukas), and listen to the original ballet music, https://www.youtube.com/watch?v=Vmh3A7ohFnc&list=RDVmh3A7ohFnc&start_radio=1&t=265. Does it evoke similar feelings?
- Purchase a 360-degree camera like the Samsung Gear 360, https://www.samsung.com/global/galaxy/gear-360/ and learn how to create your own 360 videos as a medium for storytelling and VR where the viewer has more agency over their experience.

Lesson Guide: Can VR Enhance Our Understanding of Characters in a Narrative?

Manifest 99 VR

Designed by Craig Frehlich B.Ed., M.Ed.

© 2019 Springboard Virtual Reality, Inc.

Target Age: 10-adult, Grade 5 and up	Target Subject/Field: Language Arts/ Narrative, Story-telling	Essential Idea: How we relate to characters in a story can be controlled by the author's choices.

Goal of the Learning Application:
Characterization is a crucial part of making a story compelling. Characterization can be direct or indirect in a story. MANIFEST 99 is an ominous and eerie VR story set on a train rumbling through the afterlife. Accompanied by a murder of crows and four mysterious travel companions, you must uncover the reason why they – and you – are on this train travelling into the great beyond. Gaze into their eyes and discover the remnants of their weary souls before they pass on. Can this VR application with its unique mechanics and affordances enhance your understanding of the characters?

Possible Learning Objectives:	Key Concepts & Vocabulary:
• Students will be able to analyze the impact of the author's choices regarding how characters are introduced and developed in a narrative. • Students will be able to describe character development. • Students will be able to compare and contrast different character types.	• Point-of-view • Relationship • Perspective • Persona • Transformation • Trust • Protagonist • Antagonist

Pre-Application Guidelines & Questions:
Before entering the VR application, users should answer the following questions.
- What is the difference between a protagonist and an antagonist in a story?
- The author may use several strategies to help us understand a character. Watch this video to learn more about characterization, https://www.youtube.com/watch?v=-ZnD0AGqQ7I. Which indirect technique do you feel makes it easiest to understand a character?
- Watch this video about how VR is an empathy machine, https://www.ted.com/talks/chris_milk_how_virtual_reality_can_create_the_ultimate_emp

athy_machine?language=en#t-68524. Why is VR more compelling as a new medium for telling a story?
- Perspective-taking helps us create an identity and understanding of a character. Imagination plays a more significant role in text narrative compared to the visual story. When we have not met a character, we often make assumptions about them based on interpretations and predictions. What is a persona?
- How can persona taking lead to stereotypes, racism and prejudice?

Important Tips & Tricks to Consider Inside this VR Application

What to expect? This VR narrative lasts approximately 15 minutes.

Staring into the eyes of the crow and characters will help you learn more about their identity.

Post-Application Guidelines & Reflections

Once the student/user has explored and navigated through the VR experience, they should answer the following questions:

- Describe the persona of each of the characters on the train.
- Who was the antagonist in the story?
- How was perspective established in this VR narrative?
- Why did it take several tries for the characters to reveal their story?
- To what extent did the final character in the story change or transform? What do you think caused this transformation?
- Do you think the bear, owl nun and deer forgave the antagonist in the end? Explain.
- Was it easier to establish personas in VR than through text-based narratives? Explain.
- Being empathetic towards a person or character is essential in society to increase harmony and social unity in a world filled with diversity. Have a look at this video clip, https://www.youtube.com/watch?v=dTVeXAcBlGw. To what extent do you think this VR application could promote positive relationships?
- Using VR to enhance and improve our understanding and empathy of characters by making us see things from their perspective may not always work out. For example, in VR, we might transfer our body into someone who is blind to get a better view of what it is like to live with blindness. How might this backfire?
- Understanding characters has been the goal of this learning application. Because we are human, it might be easier to have empathy and understanding toward other humans. What about animals? Stanford VR developed an app to see if people were able to create compassion toward a cow. Have a look at this video, https://www.youtube.com/watch?v=aQke1eQHSAA. Do you think it is easier to convince people to show empathy to an animal than a human? Explain.

Extension Activities
- How we see ourselves can differ from how others see us. Create a self-portrait. On the back of the self-portrait, list characteristics of yourself. Share your self-portrait with others and see if they can guess the features you listed on the back.

Lesson Guide: The Interrogation of VR Storytelling
The Great C VR

Designed by Craig Frehlich B.Ed., M.Ed.

© 2019 Springboard Virtual Reality, Inc.

Target Age:	Target Subject/Field:	Essential Idea:
13-Adult, Grade 8 and up	Language Arts, Literature/Narrative, Story-telling	To what extent are print-based stories more compelling compared to immersive VR narratives?

Goal of the Learning Application:
Are books (print-based stories) always better than movies? This has been debated in the storytelling world for many years. Proponents of books believe that text-based narratives allow us to use our imagination to build the scene and characters. But what if the film is in virtual reality? In virtual reality, the viewer is allowed to explore, look around, and gaze in multiple locations to establish a variety of perspectives. Does this new ability enhance or diminish the audience's imperative (meaning and message of the story or narrative)? Based on the sci-fi short story by Philip K. Dick, The Great C VR follows Clare, a young woman who finds her life upended when her fiancé, Tim, is summoned for this year's pilgrimage. Leaving the safe confines of her village, Clare must decide whether to accept the rules of her harsh society or fight against the oppressive powers that created it. The user will immerse themselves in this story and compare it to the print version.

Possible Learning Objectives:	Key Concepts & Vocabulary:
<ul><li>Students will be able to reflect on new understanding and its value to self and others.</li><li>Students will be able to appreciate the effectiveness and artistry of print and nonprint narratives.</li><li>Students will be able to interpret, evaluate, and effectively use different modes of communication from alternative media sources.</li><li>Students will be able to experiment with a variety of strategies, activities, and resources to explore ideas, observations, opinions, experiences, and emotions.</li></ul>	<ul><li>Imperative</li><li>Power</li><li>Perspective</li><li>Sacrifice</li><li>Dystopia</li><li>Freedom</li><li>Development</li></ul>

Pre-Application Guidelines & Questions:

Have users read the text version of the short story, The Great C, by Philip K. Dick (1953), which can be found here, http://www.isfdb.org/cgi-bin/title.cgi?2302586.
- In the short story, what is the SMASH?
- Why must Tim Meredith travel to the Great C with three questions?
- Why is Meredith so surprised that the Great C can answer his questions?
- Knowledge is Power. How does the statement apply to the short story of The Great C?
- Define the term dystopia.
- To what extent do you believe this short story is dystopian?
- Do you think our society might ever reach the situation portrayed by Philip K. Dick? Explain.

Important Tips & Tricks to Consider Inside this VR Application

What to expect? This VR narrative lasts approximately 37 minutes.

When you enter this VR application, you have some setting choices. The viewer may want to opt for the full-motion cinematic experience to get the most perspective.

Post-Application Guidelines & Reflections

Once the student/user has explored and navigated through the VR experience, they should answer the following questions:

- The VR version of The Great C is an adaptation of the print-based short story. List some similarities and differences between the print version and the VR version.
- Why was there so much death and destruction at the start of the VR story?
- The compass seems to be an important symbol or artefact in the Great C. What is its significance?
- Fear is an essential emotion in this VR narrative. How does the Great C propagate fear in humans?
- In the VR version, How did Clare end up tricking the Great C?
- In what ways is VR narrative different than regular filmmaking?
- "The Great C is just another machine made by man." Why is this quote significant?
- As our current world progress more and more toward automation, how can humans ensure that something like The Great C does not happen to us?
- Is storytelling in immersive VR more or less compelling than print-based stories? Justify and explain your position.

Extension Activities

- Purchase a 360-degree camera like the Samsung Gear 360, https://www.samsung.com/global/galaxy/gear-360/ and learn how to create your own 360 videos as a medium for storytelling and VR where the viewer has more agency over their experience.
- Watch this video clip about VR filmmaking, https://www.youtube.com/watch?v=aVwxmNqRS0Q. Answer the following questions; What did you see? What did it make you think about? What did it make you wonder about?
- Journalism is another form of storytelling. VR journalism immerses the viewer in a way that journalistic reporting can't quite achieve. For instance, the viewer experiences the event for themselves rather than having a reporter narrate it to them. Investigate the potential of VR journalism as a tool to combat "Fake News."

Appendix E

Lesson Guide: The Domino Effect of Storytelling
The Kessler Effect VR

Designed by Craig Frehlich B.Ed., M.Ed.

© 2019 Springboard Virtual Reality, Inc.

Target Age: 12-Adult, Grade 7 and up	Target Subject/Field: Literature, Language Arts/Narrative, Story-telling	Essential Idea: How we relate to a narrative can be very personal. Can giving a viewer more significant interaction and agency enhance a user's experience?
Goal of the Learning Application: Traditional stories and narratives are usually linear. The author leads us down a path or journey from point "A" to point "B." In this case, there is a high level of control over what the reader or participant sees and feels. What if there was more choice in how we experience a story or narrative? More choice might lead to higher levels of personalization and agency, thus putting the audience at the centre of a visceral experience. Does this lead to greater enjoyment? The Kessler Effect is the first interactive VR movie where you become the main hero of a thrilling sci-fi adventure and can influence the development of the plot and its ending.		
Possible Learning Objectives: • Students will be able to appreciate the effectiveness and artistry of nonprint narratives like VR story-telling. • Students will explore what effect choice and the increased agency have on audience viewing experiences. • Students will be able to experiment with a variety of strategies and resources to explore experiences and emotions. (ie. audio clues, haptics and visual effects). • Students will be able to interpret, evaluate and effectively use different modes of communication from alternative media sources like VR story-telling.		**Key Concepts & Vocabulary:** • Causality • Agency • Free-will • Fate • Time and Space

Pre-Application Guidelines & Questions:

Before entering the VR application, users should answer the following questions.
- Some people like to map out their travel plans before they go on vacation. When you go on a vacation, do you have a plan for each day, or do you go with the flow and let the experience happen? Explain. Which do you prefer?
- Recently, Netflix created a unique viewing experience, Black Mirror Bandersnatch. Watch this video, https://www.youtube.com/watch?v=rPc722CSYwU. This kind of narrative blurs the lines between story and game. How is this type of viewing exercise different than a regular tv episode?
- Watch this video clip, https://www.youtube.com/watch?v=7gKj0mokwqc. What are some advantages of watching a "choose your own adventure" video? What are some disadvantages?
- Giving the viewer greater control and agency can help personalize our viewing experience. Customizing the story and narrative can lead to multiple points of view regarding the message intended for the story. What are some things that might not change in a "choose your own adventure"?

Important Tips & Tricks to Consider Inside this VR Application

What to expect? This VR narrative will take approximately 20 minutes.

In this narrative, you play the role of Aurora, an artificial intelligence robotic pilot. Along with your trusted mechanic, Green, you are faced with hard choices about saving the universe.

Post-Application Guidelines & Reflections

Once the student/user has explored and navigated through the VR experience, they should answer the following questions:

- Describe some ways you were able to have more control or agency over the story or narrative beyond a traditional tale.
- Why do you think the authors of this narrative gave it the title, "The Kessler Effect"?
- What is the Domino effect? How does it apply to this story or narrative?
- In what ways did you feel like you were at the centre of the action?
- What are some alternative plot-lines or endings to the story?
- What is causality, and how does it impact the story?
- Try the story again and come up with an alternative plot-line and ending. Which one did you like better? Why?
- Many movies play with the idea of cause and effect. If we could go back in time, might we be able to alter our future? What do you believe?
- If you could re-live part of your life again, what part would it be, and what might you do to alter the ending?

Extension Activities

- Watch the 1993 comedy, Groundhog Day. You can view the trailer here, https://www.youtube.com/watch?v=tSVeDx9fk60. How is Groundhog Day similar to the Kessler Effect? How is it different?
- Compare this type of VR narrative to others that are present on the SpringboardVR platform like The Great C and Firebird LaPeri. How are they similar and different?

Appendix E

Lesson Guide: A Journey through Bipolar Disorder
Manic VR

Designed by Craig Frehlich B.Ed., M.Ed.

© 2019 Springboard Virtual Reality, Inc.

Target Age:	Target Subject/Field:	Essential Idea:
12-Adult, Grade 7 and up	Language Arts, Health and Wellness/ Narrative, Story-telling, Mental Health	To what extent are we shaped by our actions and those of others? What impacts our overall mental health?

Goal of the Learning Application:

Struggling with a mental illness can be hard as it often affects the people around us. Our mental health is shaped by beliefs, memories, expectations, hopes and experiences. It has been said that we are a total of the decisions we make in a lifetime. Freedom of choice is a blurry topic in the 21st century. Who governs our choices? Parents, friends, family and algorithms influence our mechanism of choice and, therefore, our changing identity. In this VR application, we explore this idea in the mind of a person struggling with bipolar disorder. Manic VR immerses participants in the exuberant and chaotic worlds of an imagination haunted by bipolar disorder. Through room-scale, real-time interaction and 3D worlds, the user will discover the destabilizing effects of bipolarity – the heightening of senses and the untamed imagination that accompanies this complex and mysterious condition. As the user watches this immersive story play out, they will reflect on how our decisions shape our mental health and identity.

Possible Learning Objectives:	Key Concepts & Vocabulary:
<ul><li>Students will be able to understand and identify facets of their identities.</li><li>Students will be able to explore what aspects affect and change our mental health.</li><li>Students will be able to interpret, evaluate and effectively use different modes of communication from alternative media sources.</li><li>Students will be able to reflect on new understanding and its value to self and others.</li></ul>	<ul><li>Freedom-of-choice</li><li>Algorithms</li><li>Bipolar Disorder</li><li>Identity</li><li>Mental Health</li></ul>

Pre-Application Guidelines & Questions:

Before entering the VR application, users should answer the following questions.
- What is bipolar disorder?
- There are a lot of pressures in today's society regarding how we behave and make decisions. People around us may have certain expectations that can stress our mental

Appendix E

health. Alas, to add to the pressure is the role that online algorithms play in shaping our lives. Have a look at this video, https://www.youtube.com/watch?v=ENWVRcMGDoU. What are some advantages of using algorithms in our life? What are some disadvantages?
- Our interactions online can shape our identity. Have a look at this experiment by Microsoft, https://www.youtube.com/watch?v=Lr4yi9onykg. Why did Microsoft shut down the chatbot, Tay?
- Besides reflecting on how we make decisions online, what are some other ways we can improve our mental health?

Important Tips & Tricks to Consider Inside this VR Application

What to expect? This VR experience is approximately 10 minutes long. Pay close attention to the variety of techniques used by the author to immerse the listener into the story.

Post-Application Guidelines & Reflections

Once the student/user has explored and navigated through the VR experience, they should answer the following questions:

- Describe what makes this VR narrative story about the struggles with bipolar disorder more powerful than a standard video.
- What were some clues within the VR experience that indicated the main character was depressed?
- Why is Manic an appropriate title for the VR story?
- Hearing voices in your head can be a symptom of bipolar disorder. Who were some of the voices in this narrative?
- Besides extreme emotional lows, bipolar sufferers also experience intense emotional highs. Give an example of a scene that depicted this in the VR application.
- What were some indications that the bipolar sufferer in the narrative was struggling with decision making?
- There is a theory that you can control depression by surrounding yourself with positive people and positivity. Have a look at this video, https://www.youtube.com/watch?v=-miTTiaqFll. Do you agree that we should live without the news?

Extension Activities
- Nurture vs Nature. Some diseases are more prevalent as a result of genetic dispositions and are passed on from one family member to another through inheritance. However, some are controlled by our environment and the people we surround ourselves with every day. Research Bipolar disorder and write a report explaining whether the disease is more influenced by nurture (our environment) or nature (our genetics).
- SpringboardVR has an application on its portal to improve our mental health. Try out Nature Treks VR. Additionally, several websites aim to reduce our stress and anxiety in a busy world. Calm offers free membership for students and educations, https://www.calm.com/schools.

Appendix E

Lesson Guide: Exploring Our Changing Identity
In Memory

Designed by Craig Frehlich B.Ed., M.Ed.

© 2019 Springboard Virtual Reality, Inc.

Target Age: 10-Adult, Grade 5 and up	Target Subject/Field: Language Arts/Narrative, Story-telling	Essential Idea: To what extent can tragedy alter our identity

Goal of the Learning Application:
Our self-concept or identity is shaped by beliefs, memories, expectations, hopes and experiences. Furthermore, it provides people with a sense of worth and a lens through which they look at the world. There are many things that might change or alter our identity. In this VR application, we explore this idea. Locked away in a cold, dark prison cell with no hope of getting released any time soon, all that Jedrick has left are the most precious memories of his beloved: a means to escape from his grim reality. In this short story made exclusively for VR, the mental escape of Jedrick becomes a physical one as you literally step into his memories and learn Jedrick's story.

Possible Learning Objectives:	Key Concepts & Vocabulary:
• Students will be able to reflect on facets of their personal identities. • Students will be able to explore what aspects affect and change our identity. • Students will be able to interpret, evaluate and effectively use different modes of communication from alternative media sources.	• Identity • Dualism • Change • Perspective • Point of View

Pre-Application Guidelines & Questions:
Before entering the VR application, users should answer the following questions.
- Superheroes like Spiderman, Batman and Superman often struggle with dual identities. Watch this trailer related to Spiderman 2, https://www.youtube.com/watch?v=aR9osGLmlkY. It is sometimes hard being two people at once. Yet, giving up our identity for something new and different can also be a struggle. What shapes our identity?
- Why do superheroes often struggle with their identities?
- How can memories help maintain our identity?
- What are false memories, and how might they influence our identity?
- Describe an event in your life that was difficult. Did it change your identity? Explain.
- What are some ways we can preserve our memories?

Appendix F

VR Lesson Guides for Health, Physical Education, and Wellness

Lesson Guide: VR as an Exercise Machine
Audioshield

Designed by Craig Frehlich B.Ed., M.Ed.

© 2019 Springboard Virtual Reality, Inc.

Target Age: 11+, Grade 5 and up	Target Subject/Field: Health and Physical Education	Essential Idea: To what extent can VR applications increase our enjoyment of exercise?
Goal of the Learning Application: Getting regular exercise for some people can be a struggle because it sometimes makes us uncomfortable when we push the physiological limits of our bodies. Having a distraction like listening to podcasts, watching television, a movie or participating with others in a group can sometimes distract us from the pain and discomfort induced by exercise. Some immersive VR applications have been designed to make us active during game-play. In these situations, painless minutes pass by without our brain even knowing we have increased our heart rate. Audioshield is a fast-paced game that challenges the user to block the beats. Audioshield puts the user at the point of impact for every hit in the songs. Participants block incoming orbs with shields and move around in the process. Can an active VR application like Audioshield increase our enjoyment of exercise while still maintaining a high enough threshold of activity to qualify as regular exercise?		
Possible Learning Objectives:<ul><li>Students will understand, experience and appreciate the health benefits that result from physical activity.</li><li>Students will be able to apply and refine non-locomotor skills and concepts to a variety of activities with increased control to improve personal performance.</li><li>Students will be able to analyze, evaluate and adapt the performance of non-locomotor skills and concepts—effort, space, and relationships—to perform and create a variety of activities to improve personal performance.</li><li>Students will be able to select and perform simple movement sequences by using elements of body and space awareness and relationships.</li></ul>		**Key Concepts & Vocabulary:**<ul><li>Personality</li><li>Fitness</li><li>Systems</li><li>Development</li><li>Time, Space and Place</li><li>Identity</li><li>Perspective</li></ul>

Pre-Application Guidelines & Questions:

Watch this video before answering the questions,
https://www.youtube.com/watch?v=_TTV5lHpcOo.
- Is regular exercise laborious for you? Why or why not?
- What types of exercise do you enjoy most? Least?
- What types of distractions (i.e., music, TV, movies, group exercise) have you used to increase your motivation and engagement in regular exercise?
- If exercise was more like a game, would you enjoy it more? Explain why or why not.

Important Tips & Tricks to Consider Inside this VR Application

What to expect?

Before the user enters Audioshield, they will need some way to monitor their exercise. Have the participant wear a fitness tracker like a Fitbit or Apple watch that counts steps and measures heart rate.

When the user enters the VR application, they are asked to customize various settings like the shape of their shield, difficulty level, and type of music. It is recommended that the user pick "Harder" for the difficulty level to ensure they have to move at a high enough rate. Users may want to watch this video as an introduction before they play,
https://www.youtube.com/watch?v=dvSpWPcH5JI.

Ask participants to play for approximately 15 minutes. When the user has finished the VR application, record the total number of steps taken in 15 minutes from their Fitbit or watch and the average heart rate (if possible).

Post-Application Guidelines & Reflections

Ask participants to exercise on a stair stepper machine for 15 minutes at about the same intensity level. If measured their average heart rate while in Audioshield, they can use this data point to get them to repeat that heart rate on the stair stepper. Now have them answer the following questions;

- Which type of experience did you enjoy more? Why?
- What was the most challenging part of playing the Audioshield game?
- Was it easy to maintain a high enough level of intensity in Audioshield to make it feel like you were exercising? Explain.
- Do you think society should embrace VR gaming as a legitimate form of exercise? Why or why not?
- Many exercise distractions like watching television has a decay rate. That is to say, the novelty wears off, and we lose the distraction effect. Do you think this will be the case for VR as an exercise machine? Explain.

Extension Activities

- Immersive VR has also been used effectively to distract patients during painful surgeries and injuries. Have a look at this video, https://www.youtube.com/watch?v=YOFPT7YTjAE. What is one thing you agreed with from the video? What is one thing you disagree with? Give one thing you did not know before watching the video. What is one thing that inspires you from watching the video?
- Try other VR applications like Beat Saber or Sprint Vector and compare and contrast your level of enjoyment and intensity of exercise to Audioshield. Which VR application gave you the most enjoyable workout? Why? Which VR application provided the most intense workout? Explain.

Lesson Guide: Can VR Enhance Our Baseball Hitting Skills?
Everyday Baseball VR
Designed by Craig Frehlich B.Ed., M.Ed.

© 2019 Springboard Virtual Reality, Inc.

Target Age:	Target Subject/Field:	Essential Idea:
10-Adult, Grade 5 and up	Health and Physical Education/Baseball	The refinement of a skill or technique involves careful consideration of the body's balance and energy transformation.

Goal of the Learning Application:

Learning a new sport requires focus, practice, refinement and reflection. Skill development does not usually happen automatically. However, with the right emphasis on technique, body positioning and transfer of energy, beginners can hone their skills and become better at any sport. In this VR application, you will reflect on your baseball hitting skills and technique. Can this type of VR experience enhance our baseball skills?

Possible Learning Objectives:	Key Concepts & Vocabulary:
<ul><li>Students will be able to reflect on their learning experiences in the field of baseball.</li><li>Students will be able to use inquiry to explore the physical techniques related to hitting a baseball.</li><li>Students will be able to practice focus and concentration.</li><li>Students will be able to demonstrate and apply a range of strategies and movement concepts.</li><li>Students will be able to demonstrate and apply a range of skills and techniques effectively as they relate to hitting a baseball.</li><li>Students will be able to analyze and evaluate performance.</li></ul>	<ul><li>Technique</li><li>Movement</li><li>Repetition</li><li>Transformation</li><li>Balance</li><li>Refinement</li></ul>

Appendix F 115

Pre-Application Guidelines & Questions:

Before entering the VR application, users should answer the following questions.
- Watch this video on the science behind hitting a baseball, https://www.youtube.com/watch?v=RENLMum5wz4. What are some advantages or traits needed for humans to be good at hitting a baseball?
- Watch this video, https://www.youtube.com/watch?v=7JSMEOv4dXQ. What are the seven steps to hitting a baseball? Which of these steps was difficult for you to understand?
- Rhythm and timing are vital to be a capable hitter in baseball. Have a look at this video about how to improve your rhythm and timing, https://www.youtube.com/watch?v=7JSMEOv4dXQ. What does "load" refer to in the video, and why is it important?
- Where we contact the ball on the bat is essential in baseball. The player should ensure they touch the ball in the "fat part" of the bat. This VR application gives you feedback on where the ball hit the bat after each pitch. Why is contact on this part of the bat important?
- The angle of our bat is critical when we contact the baseball. If we attack the ball with too much of an upper swing, the ball may "pop-up," and if we swing down on the ball, it may end up as a rolling ball on the ground, which can easily be fielded. The optimum attack angle should be slightly up, as explained in this video, https://www.youtube.com/watch?v=6WmYX3NZlWM. Why is it so essential to get a good attack angle when we hit the ball?
- Hitting the ball in various locations on the field is an essential strategy. Productive hitters can hit to the right, left and middle part of the field with the right timing and technique. If a pitch is on the inside of the plate, the best way to approach this type of pitch is to pull the ball (if you are a right-handed hitter, this means hitting the ball to the left-field). If the pitch is on the outside of the plate, it might be strategic to hit the ball to the opposite field (if you are a right-handed hitter, this means hitting the ball to the right-field). Have a look at this video, https://www.youtube.com/watch?v=Z7IigyDM1tc. Besides hitting an outside pitch to the right-field, where else might be an acceptable location to hit an outside pitch?

Important Tips & Tricks to Consider Inside this VR Application

What to expect? Allow the user to spend 15- 20 minutes in the VR application.

The user will practice hitting baseballs in 3-minute intervals. Users should work on practicing various skills based on the questions and videos in the pre-application section of this guide. For example, users should practice hitting balls to multiple parts of the field (right, left and centre). Furthermore, users should practice swinging the bat at the right attack angle to ensure they are not popping the ball up or hitting grounders. Additionally, users should pay close attention to where they are contacting the ball on the bat.

Post-Application Guidelines & Reflections

Once the student/user has explored and navigated through the VR experience, they should answer the following questions:

- Did your overall score improve as you progressed through the game? Why or why not?
- Where you stand in the batter's box can vary depending on the needs of the hitter. Describe what your strategy was in regards to where you stood in the batter's box.

- Hitting different kinds of pitches can be a challenge. This pitcher sometimes would throw fastballs, big slow curve balls and medium speed pitches. Which type of pitch did you prefer? Why?
- Which aspect of hitting did you find the most difficult to improve:
  - Hitting the ball on the "fat" part of the bat?
  - Hitting the ball to different parts of the field?
  - Hitting the ball with an optimal attack angle?
- Although this VR game seems realistic, what are some limitations to this application compared to real baseball hitting?
- Have a look at this video, https://www.youtube.com/watch?v=PToEedE3H6k&t=282s. How are baseball players in this video clip using VR to improve their performance?
- If you were able to re-design this VR application, what features would you add to enhance its abilities to develop batting skills?
- Do you feel this application helped improve your baseball hitting skills? Explain why or why not?

Extension Activities

- This virtual pitching simulator, https://www.youtube.com/watch?v=f-QEvTaWoaM, came out around 1993 as an interactive baseball training tool. To what extent is this type of technology more or less effective than a VR baseball application?
- SpringboardVR has several other sports applications to strengthen your skills. Try out one of the following VR experiences to see if you can enhance your athletic skills; Tennis Kings VR, Everyday Golf VR and Hoops VR.

Appendix F

Lesson Guide: Can VR Help Refine Our Athletic Skills?
Everyday Golf VR
Designed by Craig Frehlich B.Ed., M.Ed.

© 2019 Springboard Virtual Reality, Inc.

Target Age:	Target Subject/Field:	Essential Idea:
10-adult, Grade 5 and up	Sports, Health and Physical Education/ Golf	The refinement of a skill or technique involves careful consideration of the body's balance and energy transformation.

Goal of the Learning Application:
Learning a new sport requires focus, practice, refinement and reflection. Skill development does not usually happen automatically. However, with the right emphasis on technique, body positioning and transfer of energy, beginners can hone their skills and become better at any sport. In this VR application, you will reflect on your golf skills. Everyday Golf VR offers realistic gameplay along with diagnostic tools like wing analysis and swing trajectory to help a user refine their golf skills.

Possible Learning Objectives:	Key Concepts & Vocabulary:
<ul><li>Students will be able to reflect on their learning experiences in the sport of golf.</li><li>Students will be able to use inquiry to explore the physical techniques related to hitting a golf ball.</li><li>Students will be able to practice focus and concentration.</li><li>Students will be able to demonstrate and apply a range of strategies and movement concepts.</li><li>Students will be able to demonstrate and apply a range of skills and techniques effectively as they relate to hitting a golf ball.</li><li>Students will be able to analyze and evaluate performance.</li><li>Students will be able to adapt their golf swing and strategy to various wind conditions.</li></ul>	<ul><li>Technique</li><li>Movement</li><li>Repetition</li><li>Transformation</li><li>Balance</li><li>Refinement</li><li>Adaptation</li></ul>

Appendix F

Pre-Application Guidelines & Questions:

Before entering the VR application, users should answer the following questions.

- The basic mechanics of a golf swing can be found here, https://www.youtube.com/watch?v=sXtekwuT8R0. What was one of the most important "take-aways" from watching this video?
- Putting is another vital stroke in the game of golf. Have a look at this video, https://www.youtube.com/watch?v=ITRaVI6lDPE. What are the most important things to remember when putting? What is the advantage of putting this way?
- How to set up to swing our club has to do with our stance. Have a look at this video, https://www.youtube.com/watch?v=ITRaVI6lDPE. How is your set-up and stance for hitting an iron different than when you hit with the driver?
- Wind may be a factor in this VR application. There are many ways to adjust for the wind depending on which direction the wind is going. Watch this video to learn how to play your shots when we are shooting into the wind, https://www.youtube.com/watch?v=ITRaVI6lDPE. What are some other tips for shooting a golf shot with a crosswind and a tailwind?

Important Tips & Tricks to Consider Inside this VR Application

What to expect?

The user should spend about 7- 10 minutes in the practice section of the golf application. In this area, they should work on taking golf shots using various clubs with an emphasis on club angle and trajectory, stance, as well as hand and head positioning. Additionally, the user should practise their putting technique.

This VR application has a golf swing analysis. The user should pay attention to how this works for a few swings.

Next, the user should enter the SINGLE PLAYER area. They will be required to practice short par three courses for the first nine holes and then will have the opportunity to unlock and play longer holes after the first nine short holes. While playing in the SINGLE PLAYER area, users should work on golf swing techniques as well as reading the wind conditions.

Post-Application Guidelines & Reflections

Once the student/user has explored and navigated through the VR experience, they should answer the following questions:

- Did you improve as you progressed through the VR application? Why or why not?
- Which part of your golf game did you find was the strongest, driving the ball, iron play, or putting?
- This application has a golf swing analysis. What things did you learn both positive or negative by using the golf swing analysis?
- Although this VR experience seems realistic, what were some limitations to this application compared to real golf?

- If you were able to re-design this VR application, what features would you add to enhance its abilities to develop golf skills?
- Undulating greens are more challenging to putt because the ball can move in unpredictable directions and speeds. What were some of your strategies when putting on a sloped green?

Extension Activities

- The rise of eSports has been astonishing. Many eSports participants compete for big money. However, most eSports tournaments focus on gaming programs like Dota and Fortnight. In this VR application, there is the possibility to compete against other users around the world. Do you think eSports should also start to provide serious competition for applications like Everyday Golf VR?
- SpringboardVR has several other sports applications to strengthen athletic skills. Try out one of the following VR experiences to see if you can enhance your athletic skills; Everyday Baseball VR, Tennis Kings VR and Hoops VR.

Appendix F

Lesson Guide: Can VR Help Refine Our Athletic Skills?
Tennis Kings VR
Designed by Craig Frehlich B.Ed., M.Ed.

© 2019 Springboard Virtual Reality, Inc.

Target Age:	Target Subject/Field:	Essential Idea:
10-Adult, Grade 5 and up	Sports, Health and Physical Education/ Tennis	The refinement of a skill or technique involves careful consideration of the body's balance and energy transformation.

Goal of the Learning Application:
Learning a new sport requires focus, practice, refinement and reflection. Skill development does not usually happen automatically. However, with the right emphasis on technique, body positioning and transfer of energy, beginners can hone their skills and become better at any sport. In this VR application, you will reflect on your tennis skills. Tennis Kings VR uses highly realistic physics whereby the player can compete one-on-one against the computer or a friend.

Possible Learning Objectives:	Key Concepts & Vocabulary:
• Students will be able to reflect on their learning experiences in the sport of tennis. • Students will be able to use inquiry to explore the physical techniques related to hitting a tennis ball. • Students will be able to practice focus and concentration. • Students will be able to demonstrate and apply a range of strategies and movement concepts. • Students will be able to demonstrate and apply a range of skills and techniques effectively as they relate to hitting a tennis ball. • Students will be able to analyze and evaluate performance.	• Technique • Movement • Repetition • Transformation • Balance • Refinement

Appendix F

Pre-Application Guidelines & Questions:

Before entering the VR application, users should answer the following questions.

- Have a look at this video, https://www.youtube.com/watch?v=ZsDd-nKwWvU. What are the five techniques that a user should focus on for an effective forehand? Which of the methods do you think will be the most difficult to get better at?
- Have a look at this video, https://www.youtube.com/watch?v=hKSr14cUn9Q. What are the three techniques for an effective one-handed backhand? Which of the methods do you think will be the most difficult to master?
- Serving is a big part of tennis. An effective tennis serve requires timing and good hand-eye coordination. Have a look at this video, https://www.youtube.com/watch?v=CkRHH2TRVAU. What were the four tips provided in the video to improve your serve? Which advice do you think will be easiest to master?
- Tennis has a unique way of keeping score. Describe the scoring system in tennis.
- Like most sports, tennis has several rules regarding gameplay. List as many tennis rules as you can think of.

Important Tips & Tricks to Consider Inside this VR Application

What to expect? Allow the user to play this VR application for approximately 15- 20 minutes.

When the user first enters the VR application, they are allowed to pick several settings like the type of racket and who they want to play against. It is suggested that the user competes against the computer AI. During gameplay, the user should focus on proper technique for forehand, backhand and serve.

Post-Application Guidelines & Reflections

Once the student/user has explored and navigated through the VR experience, they should answer the following questions:

- Did you improve as you progressed through the matches? Why or why not?
- Footwork and positioning are essential in tennis. This application allows the user to "cheat" a bit in regards to footwork. Describe how this was done in the VR application.
- Which did you find to be more effective, your forehand, backhand, or serve? Why?
- Although this VR game seems realistic, what were some limitations to this application compared to real tennis?
- If you were able to re-design this VR application, what features would you add to enhance its abilities to develop a person's tennis skills?
- Have a look at this video, which talks about the lower upper body movement in VR, https://www.youtube.com/watch?v=WjpO1m1IJxE. Do you think VR tennis can offer a good workout? Explain.

Extension Activities

- The rise of E-sports has been astonishing. Many E-sports participants compete for big money. However, most E-sports tournaments focus on gaming programs like Dota and Fortnight. In this VR application, there is the possibility to compete against other users around the world. Do you think E-sports should also start to provide serious competition for applications like Tennis Kings VR?
- SpringboardVR has several other sports applications to strengthen athletic skills. Try out one of the following VR experiences to see if you can enhance your athletic skills; Everyday Baseball VR, Everyday Golf VR and Hoops VR.

Appendix F

Lesson Guide: VR as a Tool for Safe Anonymous Introspection
Where Thoughts Go
Designed by Craig Frehlich B.Ed., M.Ed.

© 2019 Springboard Virtual Reality, Inc.

Target Age:	**Target Subject/Field:**	**Essential Idea:**
13-Adult, Grade 8 and up	Interdisciplinary, Homeroom, Advisor/Mindfulness, Psychology	Anonymity plays a crucial role in creating a safe space that compels people to open up, share, and grow emotionally.

Goal of the Learning Application:
Sharing intimate thoughts, feelings, and emotions can be very cathartic but not always easy in the real world without the help of a trusted professional psychiatrist. What if VR could provide affordances that engendered a safe place for us to do this? Can immersive VR offer emotional release and growth through thoughtful introspection? Where Thoughts Go aims to give users a safe space free from trolling, negativity, and judgment to allow users to share audio experiences based on provocative questions about life. By the end of the VR experience, the user may become more self-aware of their journey in life.

Possible Learning Objectives:	**Key Concepts & Vocabulary:**
<ul><li>Students will be able to practice empathy.</li><li>Students will learn to take responsibility for one's actions.</li><li>Students will be able to advocate for one's rights and needs.</li><li>Students will be able to practice strategies to develop mental quiet.</li><li>Students will be able to practice strategies to reduce anxiety.</li><li>Students will be able to practice strategies to prevent and eliminate bullying.</li></ul>	<ul><li>Self-awareness</li><li>Trolling/Bullying</li><li>Pain</li><li>Empathy</li><li>Loss</li><li>Resilience</li><li>Cultivating Trust</li></ul>

Pre-Application Guidelines & Questions:

Have students listen to this 12-minute episode from the Podcast "This American Life" which tells the story of how a kindergarten teacher uses a "tattle phone" to enable young children to express their frustrations, https://www.thisamericanlife.org/672/no-fair/prologue-2 (warning, this episode contains swear words, you can download the "edited" version here, https://www.thisamericanlife.org/672/no-fair).

- Why can sharing our thoughts be very relieving and cathartic (useful for our mental health)?
- It is sometimes difficult to share our personal stories online because of internet trolls. What is a "troll"?
- Give some strategies to minimize the emotional damage that can be caused by online trolls
- Sharing our stories requires trust. How do we know when to trust a friend with our personal stories?
- After we share our personal and emotional stories, we often expect things to change. Give an account of when nothing changed after doing this? How did you feel?

Important Tips & Tricks to Consider Inside this VR Application

What to expect? This VR application lasts approximately 20 minutes, depending on how many story bubbles you listen to.

When you first enter the VR application, there is a tutorial on how to navigate, listen to story bubbles, and record your personal stories. Listening to other people's responses or stories to the various questions is beneficial to form your thoughts and feelings.

Post-Application Guidelines & Reflections

Once the student/user has explored and navigated through the VR experience, they should answer the following questions:

- Which question was the easiest for you to personally respond to? Why?
- Which question was the most difficult for you to respond to? Why?
- Size and scale can be used to mitigate or minimize power and create a softer experience for users. Explain why the thought bubbles were shaped the way they were?
- What design principles have been put into place in this VR application to prevent people from trolling and harassment?
- "You are the hero of your journey." How does this quote relate to this VR application?
- Having control or agency over our experience can also promote trust. List some ways the designer of this experience built a safe space through the user's control.
- Sometimes time gives us better introspective thoughts. Think back to your answers to the questions. Pick one that you would change now that you have had more time to reflect. What did you say and how would it be different now that you have had time to think?

Extension Activities

- How we behave online is called digital citizenship. The documentary Screenagers is a compelling story about our online behavior. Here is the trailer, https://www.youtube.com/watch?v=kJPdQaOQZho. Watch the full version of Screenagers and write a report about how youth might find balance in their lives with the online world and the physical world.

Appendix F

Lesson Guide: Can VR Help Refine Our Athletic Skills?
Badminton Kings VR

Designed by Craig Frehlich B.Ed., M.Ed.

© 2019 Springboard Virtual Reality, Inc.

Target Age:	Target Subject/Field:	Essential Idea:
10-adult, Grade 5 and up	Sports, Health and Physical Education/ Tennis	The refinement of a skill or technique involves careful consideration of the body's balance and energy transformation.

Goal of the Learning Application:

Learning a new sport requires focus, practice, refinement and reflection. Skill development does not usually happen automatically. However, with the right emphasis on technique, body positioning and transfer of energy beginners can hone their skills and become better at any sport. In this VR application, you will reflect on your badminton skills. Realistic physics, immersive sound, and fluid animation make you feel like you're really in the badminton court. With physics designed to be as real as ever achieved in a badminton simulator, you will forget you are in a VR environment.

Possible Learning Objectives:	Key Concepts & Vocabulary:
<ul><li>Students will be able to reflect on their learning experiences in the sport of badminton.</li><li>Students will be able to use inquiry to explore the physical techniques related to hitting a badminton birdie.</li><li>Students will be able to practice focus and concentration.</li><li>Students will be able to demonstrate and apply a range of strategies and movement concepts.</li><li>Students will be able to demonstrate and apply a range of skills and techniques effectively as they related to hitting a badminton birdie.</li><li>Students will be able to analyze and evaluate performance.</li></ul>	<ul><li>Technique</li><li>Movement</li><li>Repetition</li><li>Transformation</li><li>Balance</li><li>Refinement</li></ul>

Appendix F

Pre-Application Guidelines & Questions:
Before entering the VR application, users should answer the following questions.
- Watch this video about the basic rules of badminton, https://www.youtube.com/watch?v=UyLIi-TbcFc. List 5 important rules.
- Have a look at this video to learn the basic mechanics of a proper badminton swing, https://www.youtube.com/watch?v=FCfq_WjWfsM. Describe the different types of badminton swings or shots.
- There are two types of serves used in badminton. Have a look at this video, https://www.youtube.com/watch?v=P5Fo9X2CHMM. Describe then you would use each type of serve.
- Besides high clear shots to the back of the court, there are also drop shots. Have a look at this video about drop shots, https://www.youtube.com/watch?v=VKN4CofsoO0. What are the two types of drop shots.
- Besides high clear shots, there are also smash shots. Have a look at this video about smash shots, https://www.youtube.com/watch?v=BnnYw0Q6YO0. List three tips for effectively hitting a smash shot.

Important Tips & Tricks to Consider Inside this VR Application

What to expect? Allow the user to play this VR application for approximately 15- 20 minutes.

When the user first enters the VR application they are allowed to pick several settings like the type of racket and who they want to play against. It is suggested that the user compete against the computer AI. During gameplay, the user should focus on proper technique for forehand, backhand and serve.

Post-Application Guidelines & Reflections

Once the student/user has explored and navigated through the VR experience, they should answer the following questions:

- Did you improve as you progressed through the matches? Why or why not?
- Footwork and positioning are essential in badminton. This application allows the user to "cheat" a bit in regards to footwork. Describe how this was done in the VR application.
- Which did you find to be more effective, your forehand clear shot, backhand clear shot, dropshot, smash shot, or serve? Why?
- Although this VR game seems realistic, what were some limitations to this application compared to real badminton?
- If you were able to re-design this VR application, what features would you add to enhance its abilities to develop a person's badminton skills?

Extension Activities
- The rise of E-sports has been astonishing. Many E-sports participants compete for big money. However, most E-sports tournaments focus on gaming programs like Dota and Fortnight. In this VR application, there is the possibility to compete against other users around the world. Do you think E-sports should also start to provide serious competition for applications like Badminton Kings VR?
- SpringboardVR has several other sports applications to strengthen athletic skills. Try out one of the following VR experiences to see if you can enhance your athletic skills; Everyday Baseball VR, Everyday Golf VR and Hoops VR.

Appendix F

Lesson Guide: VR as a Tool for Mindfulness and Meditation
Nature Treks VR

Designed by Craig Frehlich B.Ed., M.Ed.

© 2019 Springboard Virtual Reality, Inc.

Target Age: 8+, Grade 3 and up	Target Subject/Field: Interdisciplinary, Mindfulness and Stress Relief	Essential Idea: To what extent can VR be used as an effective tool to reduce stress and achieve a meditative state and promote wellness?
Goal of the Learning Application: Traditional meditation can be difficult for many people because they have to work hard at clearing the mind and focussing on calming thoughts and experiences. Can VR help expedite the relaxation process by eliminating mind-wandering thoughts that might slow down or derail the meditative thought process? In this VR application, you will be immersed in a chosen environment that helps you explore, slow down, de-stress and enjoy your tranquil surroundings. The aim is to be mindful in the moment by shutting out external distractions and escaping into a world of peace, relaxation and path toward overall wellness.		
Possible Learning Objectives: • Students will be able to practice strategies to develop mental quiet. • Students will be able to practice strategies to overcome distractions. • Students will be able to inquire in different contexts to gain a different perspective.	**Key Concepts & Vocabulary:** • Mindfulness • Connection • Meditation • Presence • Wellness	
Pre-Application Guidelines & Questions: Have students watch this TED talk about mindfulness either as an entire class or individually, https://www.youtube.com/watch?time_continue=1&v=qzR62JJCMBQ. Then, get them to discuss their impressions by answering the following questions. • What did the speaker use the juggling balls to represent in the video? • Why is it difficult for many of us to meditate? • According to the TED talk, what does it mean to be "mindful"? • Give one idea you agreed within the TED talk and one idea you disagreed with?		

Important Tips & Tricks to Consider Inside this VR Application

What to expect?

When a person enters Nature Treks they are given the opportunity to explore eight different scenes or environments. Within each environment a person can control "orbs" which affect things like the time of day, rain and snow, and being able to create trees and foliage. Make sure the user explores by walking or teleporting around in the environment until they find a place of solitude. In their place of solitude, the user should sit down and reflect, work on deep breathing and try to meditate and calm the mind. Breathing rates and/or heart rates could be monitored as an indicator of relaxation. The recommended time would be approximately 20 minutes per student.

Post-Application Guidelines & Reflections

Once the student/user has explored and navigated through the VR experience they should answer the following questions:

- What was your average resting heart rate inside the application? If this was not your first time in the application, was your average resting heart rate lower than your previous experience? Why or why not?
- Describe your "place of Solitude". How long did it take you to find this place?
- What was the name of the environment you picked to enter? Why did you choose this environment? IF you had to pick another environment which one would it be and why?
- Many advocates of immersive virtual reality claim that mindfulness is easier in VR. From your experience in this VR application do you think this is the case? Why or why not?

Extension Activities
- Mandalas are sacred circles that have been used as a meditation activity or technique. Print off a variety of Mandalas from this website http://www.mandala-4free.de/en/index.htm and distribute them to students in your class and have them practice calming techniques while they colour the circles. For example, play some mindfulness music in the background.

Appendix F

Lesson Guide: Can VR Help Refine Our Athletic Skills?
Hoops VR

Designed by Craig Frehlich B.Ed., M.Ed.

© 2019 Springboard Virtual Reality, Inc.

Target Age:	Target Subject/Field:	Essential Idea:
10-Adult, Grade 5 and up	Sports, Physical Education/Basketball Skills	The refinement of a skill or technique involves careful consideration of the body's balance and energy transformation along with thoughtful repetition.

Goal of the Learning Application:
Learning a new sport requires focus, practice, refinement and reflection. Skill development does not usually happen automatically. However, with the right emphasis on technique, body positioning and transfer of energy, beginners can hone their skills and become better at any sport. In this VR application, you will reflect on your basketball shooting skills. Hoops VR is specially designed so you can live out the ultimate basketball free-throw challenge. Use the motion controls and shoot hoops as naturally as you would out on the basketball court.

Possible Learning Objectives:	Key Concepts & Vocabulary:
<ul><li>Students will be able to reflect on their learning experiences in the field of basketball.</li><li>Students will be able to use inquiry to explore the physical techniques related to shooting a basketball.</li><li>Students will be able to practice focus and concentration.</li><li>Students will be able to demonstrate and apply a range of strategies and movement concepts.</li><li>Students will be able to demonstrate and apply a range of skills and techniques effectively as they relate to shooting a basketball.</li><li>Students will be able to analyze and evaluate performance.</li></ul>	<ul><li>Refinement</li><li>Technique</li><li>Repetition</li><li>Transformation</li><li>Balance</li><li>Movement</li></ul>

Appendix F

Pre-Application Guidelines & Questions:
Before entering the VR application, users should answer the following questions.
- Immersive VR is being used to train athletes in sports. Have a look at this video, https://www.youtube.com/watch?v=X0DFCmIJiJA, now describe some benefits and drawbacks of using VR to train athletes in sports.
- Having the right technique is key to shooting a basketball. Watch this video, https://www.youtube.com/watch?v=MuOKHVcqgD4. List several key points that the coach emphasized in the video.
- How far we shoot the ball is dependent on our transfer of energy. There are two critical areas on our body that can help players shoot basketballs further. First is the motion of our arms. Faster release of our arms usually means further distance of the ball. Second is our legs. Bending our knees and releasing the ball as a jump shot can help propel the ball further. Have a look at this article for more information on shooting technique, https://www.breakthroughbasketball.com/fundamentals/shooting-technique.html. When would you use a standing position, instead of a jumping position to shoot a basketball?
- Another important physics consideration for shooting a basketball is the trajectory of the ball. Watch this instructional video on shooting arc. What is the optimum path for shooting a basketball? Describe what your body position needs to be to have this happen.

Important Tips & Tricks to Consider Inside this VR Application

What to expect? Allow users to spend approximately 15-20 minutes in this VR application.

When the user first enters the application, they are presented with three options; beginner, expert and trash can. It is suggested that first-time players pick the beginner level. Users will have to use the trigger to bounce and throw/release the basketball. Users should review the various techniques to shooting a basketball from the questions above and work hard to employ the proper body movement in the application. Users should also consider experiencing shooting in a standing position for one round of the game and then trying jump shots for a different level. Then, alternating between the two when appropriate. Additionally, players should try and model the right arc for the trajectory of their basketball throws.

Post-Application Guidelines & Reflections

Once the student/user has explored and navigated through the VR experience, they should answer the following questions:

- Did repetition and refinement of the basketball shooting skill allow you to score higher each time?
- Which throwing technique do you feel was more accurate; standing position or jumping position? Explain why.
- When the arc of your throws was higher, did you find you were more accurate in your throws?
- To what extent does the countdown timer deter or hinder a player from focussing on proper technique?

- Hoops VR is not perfect. Describe at least three limitations to this application that make it unrealistic to the real experience of refining a basketball shot.
- Besides skill development, how else might athletes use immersive VR to increase their success in a sport?
- Do you think Hoops VR was able to provide you with adequate exercise to keep the user healthy?

Extension Activities
- The NFL is a big advocate for the potential of VR in their sport. Look at this video, https://www.youtube.com/watch?v=4xbAi_h7taw, list three ways that NFL is benefiting from VR training. What are some drawbacks?
- SpringboardVR has several other sports applications. Try out one of the following VR experiences to see if you can enhance your athletic skills; Tennis Kings VR, Everyday Golf VR and Everyday Baseball VR.

Appendix G

VR Lesson Guides for Social Studies Education

Appendix G

Lesson Guide: The Future of Transportation
Air Car VR

Designed by Craig Frehlich B.Ed., M.Ed.

© 2019 Springboard Virtual Reality, Inc.

Target Age:	Target Subject/Field:	Essential Idea:
12-Adult, Grade 7 and up	STEM/Technology	Evaluating systems related to the development of new technologies is necessary for progress.

Goal of the Learning Application:
Who is in control? As the world becomes more advanced through automation and innovations in technology, humanity needs to ensure that systems are in place to guarantee safety and efficiency. Self-driving cars, delivery drones, and robot waiters are just a few examples of how our world is advancing at a rapid pace. With all this new technological innovation is the worry that not enough people can evaluate the risks and consequences. In this VR application, you will drive a futuristic flying car around a city to consider possible outcomes and new processes. In Aircar VR the user will pilot an aircar through a futuristic cityscape and consider the ramifications of having a town filled with flying cars.

Possible Learning Objectives:	Key Concepts & Vocabulary:
<ul><li>Students will be able to apply existing knowledge to generate new ideas, products, or processes.</li><li>Students will be able to use models and simulations to explore complex systems and issues.</li><li>Students will be able to evaluate systems and applications related to advances in technology.</li></ul>	<ul><li>Systems</li><li>Development</li><li>Evaluate</li><li>Consequences</li></ul>

Pre-Application Guidelines & Questions:
Have users watch this video about how technological advancements can sometimes go wrong, https://www.youtube.com/watch?time_continue=52&v=2cSh_Wo_mcY. Have students answer the following questions;<ul><li>Why did the plane hurt so many people?</li><li>Was the pilot to blame in this situation? Explain.</li><li>How could this incident have been prevented?</li></ul>

- A similar situation occurred recently with the Boeing 787 Max planes. Watch this video, https://www.youtube.com/watch?v=DYIawJ95VU0. List similarities and differences between these two events.
- With the emergence of drones, we are getting closer and closer to having flying cars become a reality in our world. What needs to be evaluated before you think flying cars can become a viable transportation option?

Important Tips & Tricks to Consider Inside this VR Application

What to expect?

Before the application loads, you will have to set up the controller settings depending on what type of VR headset you are using. You can find information on how to set up the controllers here, https://steamcommunity.com/app/1073390. Once the application loads, you are put inside the aircar and you have control over the steering and thrust. The user should practice how to steer and then move the trust forward to move into the futuristic city. The user should fly around the city, and practice landing on the roads as well as on top of buildings Allow the user to play for approximately 20 minutes.

Post-Application Guidelines & Reflections

Once the student/user has explored and navigated through the VR experience, they should answer the following questions:

- What was the hardest part of landing your air car on the roadway?
- What improvements or changes would you make to the futuristic city to make landing on the road easier?
- You flew the aircar in a rainy, gloomy environment. Predict what it might be like to fly the aircar on a bright sunny day.
- After experiencing the aircar for a few minutes, describe some changes you would make to the form and function of the aircar to make it easier to fly around the city.
- There are roads in this application. To what extent do you think roads are necessary in a world filled with flying cars? Explain.

Extension Activities

- Flight simulators have been used to help train pilots for years. Research the benefits and drawbacks of using flight simulators to help train pilots. Write a 1-page report on your findings.
- Cognitive load is an important consideration when flying in the real world. What is the meaning of cognitive load? Pilots are usually on alert and have to make life or death decisions. Sometimes flight simulators are not an accurate representation of what can happen in the real world. This was depicted in the movie "Sully." Please watch this clip, https://www.youtube.com/watch?v=N1fVL4AQEW8. Summarize the main idea that Sully is trying to argue in this video clip about simulators.

Lesson Guide: A Miner's Life
Cave Digger VR

Designed by Craig Frehlich B.Ed., M.Ed.

© 2019 Springboard Virtual Reality, Inc.

Target Age:	Target Subject/Field:	Essential Idea:
10-14, Grade 5 and 8	Science, Geography/Minerals, Mining	Why is mining considered a hard job?

Goal of the Learning Application:
Mining used to be a fun and lucrative profession during the "gold rush" days when minerals like gold were readily available above ground. Above ground mining or Placer Mining, was safe and inexpensive. Nowadays, most precious minerals are found deep below the surface of the earth. Underground mining can be a hard life. Explosions and poor air quality are just two reasons why underground mining is so difficult. In this VR experience, the user will play the role of an underground miner and explore and discover the world of mining. Gear up with numerous unique tools and explore the town and the depths of the mountain. What does it take to make it rich as a miner? Is the risk worth the reward?

Possible Learning Objectives:	Key Concepts & Vocabulary:
• Students will be able to identify and explain the purpose of different tools and techniques used in mining the earth. • Students will be able to demonstrate methods used in the scientific study of mining the earth. • Students will understand the risks, benefits and consequences associated with mining. • Students will be able to understand the developmental impact mining has on local and global communities.	• Development • Safety • Responsibility • Identity

Pre-Application Guidelines & Questions:
Before entering the VR application, users should answer the following questions.
- What are minerals? How do they form below the earth?
- Some minerals are considered gems and are more valuable than others. Why are gems more valuable than other minerals?

Appendix G

- Rocks and minerals may have varying degrees of hardness. Have a look at this video, https://www.youtube.com/watch?v=NF_bGfjZVRQ. Why are rock and mineral hardness important to mining for minerals and gems?
- Life in an underground mine can be dirty and dangerous. Have a look at this video, https://www.youtube.com/watch?v=dzVQ-G0sfY0. Describe some positive and negative aspects of being an underground miner.
- Have a look at this video, https://www.youtube.com/watch?v=sPGFnnUv3vA. What are the dangers of being a miner?

Important Tips & Tricks to Consider Inside this VR Application

What to expect? The user should spend approximately 20 minutes in this VR application.

When you first start this VR application, you enter an elevator, which is part of a mine shaft. You have a pickaxe, and you are challenged to swing at various rocks to break away pieces in order to expose precious and valuable minerals. Be careful. Some stones are harder than others. As you collect valuables, you are sent to different levels of the mine. One-stop on the elevator is the town. Be sure to explore around to get a deeper understanding of what a mining town was all about. Additionally, as you collect minerals, you gain money and can buy more advanced tools to increase your efficiency and profitability.

Post-Application Guidelines & Reflections

Once the student/user has explored and navigated through the VR experience, they should answer the following questions:

- From your experience, describe some positive emotions associated with being a miner.
- Now that you have experienced being a miner, what are some concerns you have with being a miner?
- This VR experience gives you access to traditional tools like a pickaxe as well as some more advanced tools. What were some more advanced tools? Where they more helpful in mining for minerals? Explain.
- This VR experience tries to imitate what it might be like to mine for minerals. What are some of its limitations?
- Different coloured rocks that you hit with your axe had varying properties. What was this difference? In a real mine, there might be some rocks that are difficult to break apart. How do they solve this problem?
- In this application, miners sometimes stumble across fossils in the rocks. How do fossils form in rocks? Are they valuable to cave miners?
- Abandoned mines have become a concern around the world. Have a look at this video, https://www.youtube.com/watch?v=bAtkRNPwdPg. Why are mine hunters a concern for many countries?
- Mining can be dangerous. If there are no strict rules, training and equipment, mining can kill many people. Have a look at this video, https://www.youtube.com/watch?v=7x4ASxHIrEA. Despite the dangers, why do so many people dig for cobalt in these mines? What is the solution?

Extension Activities

- Some precious minerals, like diamonds, can be the source of conflict in a country. Diamonds are one of those polarizing products. Look at this article on Blood Diamonds, https://time.com/blood-diamonds/. Write a report or presentation on the issue of Blood Diamonds.

Appendix G

Lesson Guide: VR as an Empathy Machine
Becoming Homeless

Designed by Craig Frehlich B.Ed., M.Ed.

© 2019 Springboard Virtual Reality, Inc.

Target Age:	Target Subject/Field:	Essential Idea:
9+, Grade 4 and up	Interdisciplinary, Advisor or Pastoral Care, Humanities, Social Studies	To what extent is our personal identity a consequence of our situation (timing and/or luck)?

Goal of the Learning Application:

In this immersive virtual reality experience the user will spend days in the life of someone who can no longer afford a home. They will interact with their environment to attempt to save their home and protect themselves and their belongings as they walk in another's shoes and face the adversity of living with diminishing resources.

Possible Learning Objectives:	Key Concepts & Vocabulary:
• Students will be able to draw reasonable conclusions and generalizations. • Students will be able to revise understanding based on new information and evidence. • Students will be able to analyse complex concepts into their constituent parts and synthesize them to create new understanding. • Students will be able to use models and simulations to explore complex systems and issues.	• Causality (cause and consequence) • Choice • Identity • Empathy

Pre-Application Guidelines & Questions:

Ask students to individually reflect on the following questions:

- When we see homeless people on the street in various cities around the world how empathetic are we toward their situation?
- Some might judge them harshly and point the blame solely on the homeless person. Is their situation always their fault?

Appendix G

Show on large screen or have students watch this video, https://www.youtube.com/watch?v=vXbAsGS5Nts, and instruct them to reflect and answer the following questions:

- What is one thing you agree with from the news clip?
- What is one thing you disagree with from the news clip?
- What is one thing you did not know from the news clip?
- What is one thing that inspires you from watching the news clip?

As a class, the teacher should ask students to share their answers/ideas from the video and lead a discussion around the issue of homelessness. Once the teacher has completed the large group discussion they could survey the class based on the following questions:

- How many blame homeless people for this problem?
- How many blame others for the issue of homelessness in the city?

Important Tips & Tricks to Consider Inside this VR Application

What to expect? This is a short -5 minute experience that involves three different scenes.

- The user is set inside an apartment and has to decide what to sell because they can't pay their bills.
- The user is set inside a car and gets a sense for what it is like to live and sleep in such a horrific space.
- The user is set inside a moving bus. They must interact with different people on the bus and develop and deeper understanding of how they became homeless.

Post-Application Guidelines & Reflections

Once the student/user has explored and navigated through the VR experience they should answer the following questions:

- When asked what type of hands to pick which did you decide on and why?
- While in the apartment, what were some of the items you decided to sell and why?
- Having access to resources like food and money can make us successful in life. What specific resources were diminishing in this VR experience?
- While in the car, why was the area so messy? Give an example of a time in your life when you have lost hope or motivation to do something. How did you overcome this predicament?
- While on the bus, you were asked to juggle your attention between a personal belonging and your safety (being threatened by a man). How did that struggle feel? Explain.
- On the bus you were able to learn about the stories of others. Which person's story resonated with you most? Why?
- We often blame others when bad things happen to them, but blame the external situations when bad things happen to us. Why is it easy to blame homeless people for their situation or identity?

- What is causality? How is it related to this VR experience?
- What are some reasons why we should be more empathetic to homeless people and their situation?
- There are many ways to raise awareness to important social issues like homeless. To what extent does VR make a person more empathetic toward this issue? Explain.

Extension Activities

- Watch the 1983 movie, Trading Places, in which an upper-class commodity broker crosses paths with a homeless person and their roles are reversed. Compare and contrast how this story might relate to the "Becoming Homeless" VR experience.
- Explore this, https://www.youtube.com/watch?v=JntavOPn-fU, 360 degree video from the perspective of a homeless person and compare and contrast this medium with the immersive VR available in Becoming Homeless.

Appendix G

Lesson Guide: Firefighter Safety Training in VR
Awaken VR

Designed by Craig Frehlich B.Ed., M.Ed.

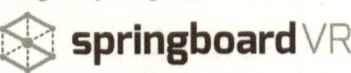

© 2019 Springboard Virtual Reality, Inc.

Target Age:	Target Subject/Field:	Essential Idea:
9+, Grade 5 and up	Science, Physics, STEM/Problem Solving, Career Training	To what extent can the form of an object function as a system for safety?

Goal of the Learning Application:
Before 1983, life nets and slides were sometimes used by firefighters as pieces of equipment to allow people on top floors of burning buildings an opportunity to escape safely to the ground. Today, these life nets are rarely used in firefighting efforts. Are life nets and slides too dangerous to be used as an effective safety device in the 21st century? In this learning experience, you will use slides and life nets (trampolines) to get a ball from one location to another without hitting the ground in order to develop a better understanding of the physics behind slides and life nets. Each level gets harder and more complex.

Possible Learning Objectives:	Key Concepts & Vocabulary:
<ul><li>Students will be able to practice observing carefully in order to recognize problems.</li><li>Students will be able to design improvements to existing complex machines or systems.</li><li>Students will be able to apply skills and knowledge in unfamiliar situations.</li><li>Students will be able to predict the direction of objects based on their angle of movement.</li></ul>	<ul><li>Form</li><li>Creativity</li><li>Connections</li><li>Systems</li><li>Safety</li></ul>

Pre-Application Guidelines & Questions:
A life net is a type of rescue equipment formerly used by firefighters. When used in the proper conditions, it allowed people on upper floors of burning buildings an opportunity to jump to safety. See this video, https://www.youtube.com/watch?v=gwOOC-8INQM . Additionally, safety slides have been used in buildings to evacuate people from upper floors. See this video, https://www.youtube.com/watch?v=ndSbtqjGz7k. Answer these questions about life nets and safety slides:

- What are the benefits to using these two types of safety devices?
- What are some drawbacks or limitations to using these two types of safety devices?
- A basic understanding of physics can help ensure the function of these two devices is error free. What physics concepts would be important to consider when using each of these devices?

Important Tips & Tricks to Consider Inside this VR Application

What to expect?

There are two modes for this VR application. One is a "creation mode" which would allow the user to design their own puzzles. The other mode is "gameplay mode" in which the user tries to solve pre-designed puzzles that increase in difficulty. The gameplay mode should be used for this VR lesson guide. In the first few minutes of this VR experience, the user is introduced to a tutorial which guides them through how to use the movement controls and how to hold, grab and manipulate objects. In the first few levels only slides and life nets (mini-trampolines) are used to guide balls to specified locations. It is recommended that the user play for approximately 20 minutes to get a sense for the experience. Users may want to watch this video before entering the VR application, https://www.youtube.com/watch?v=TPhxz1dneNk.

Post-Application Guidelines & Reflections

Once the user has played for approximately 20 minutes have them leave the VR application and answer the following questions:
- In what ways were the slides in this VR learning engagement similar to slides used as escapes for people from burning buildings? How are they different?
- In what ways were the life nets (mini-trampolines) similar to the ones used by firefighters for safety devices? How are they different?
- When you have to combine slides and life nets, why is it considerably more dangerous?
- If you were able to adapt the shape of the slides and life nets in this application what would you do differently to their form? Why?
- In the real world, life nets have been criticized for being unsafe and have been discontinued in most parts of the world? Do you agree or disagree with this decision? Justify your reasons.

Extension Activities
- VR is being used by firefighters to prepare them for emergency situations like in this video, https://www.youtube.com/watch?v=q8_A3WnTS8s and this video, https://www.youtube.com/watch?v=UINQiLfAYhY. Discuss the positives and negatives to this type of training for firefighters.
- Watch the (1991) movie, Backdraft, to get a sense of what it's like to be a firefighter and the dangers involved. You can see the trailer here, https://www.youtube.com/watch?v=dgtRBUkheYk. (Please note the movie is rated PG). Write a report on the physiological and psychological dangers to being a firefighter.

Lesson Guide: VR as a Tool for Skill Development

Modbox

Designed by Craig Frehlich B.Ed., M.Ed.

© 2019 Springboard Virtual Reality, Inc.

Target Age: 11+, Grade 6 and up	Target Subject/Field: Interdisciplinary, Health and Physical Education, General Science/Physics	Essential Idea: To what extent can VR be used to scaffold the learning of complex processes?
Goal of the Learning Application: What if we could use VR to slow cognitive and physical processes down in order to scaffold a learning experience. When we learn a new skill there is a progression of development and refinement that is followed to allow the brain to make small connections to our physical body. For example, juggling in real life takes practice and time, and thanks to gravity makes the threshold for many beginners too high to achieve mastery immediately. However, in VR we can reduce the gravity of the juggling balls and make the hand, eye and brain work together at a different pace in order to establish rhythm and technique. Modbox is an application that gives you control over the environment and allows users to create virtual worlds and environments. With the help of Modbox processes can be adjusted or differentiated to give users greater control (agency) over the scaffolding processes and enable users to achieve mastery at a quicker pace.		
Possible Learning Objectives: • Students will be able to develop new techniques and strategies for effective learning of a skill or process through refinement. (ie. juggling) • Students will be able to adapt and improve activity specific skills. • Students will be able to understand the laws of gravity and its effects on falling objects. • Students will be able to try new forms of technology and evaluate their effectiveness.	**Key Concepts & Vocabulary:** • Scaffolding • Refinement • Resilience • Development • Trial and error • Gravity	

Pre-Application Guidelines & Questions:

Rarely do people pick up something and achieve mastery right away. Have students think about a sport or hobby they have played before. When these skills are broken down into a simple step by step processes with opportunities to practice along the way students are quicker to master the skill. Additionally, the threshold of failure is lower because students are feeling incremental chunks of success and require smaller doses of resiliency. Show students this progression on how to catch the baseball to get a better understanding, https://www.youtube.com/watch?v=Ohy4hOefDx4. Then, have them answer the following questions:

- The development of a skill takes practice. With more practice comes greater mastery. Think of a time in your life when you picked up on something quickly and it required very little practice to achieve success. What was it? Explain.
- Think of a sport you played or a hobby you tried and list the step-by-step process to learning the skill within that sport/hobby. For example, how to serve a volleyball, how to shoot a slapshot in hockey, or how to tie your shoe.
- Now, try and think of a skill/talent that can't be acquired through practice. What is it? Explain how it required no practice.

Important Tips & Tricks to Consider Inside this VR Application

What to expect?

Students will use Modbox as a tool to teach them the skill of juggling. Thanks to the power of Modbox users can adjust settings like gravity in order to scaffold the development of the skill of juggling. In order for students to understand how to use Modbox as a progression tool to teach the art of juggling have them watch this video first before putting on a headset and entering Modbox, https://www.youtube.com/watch?v=7dTkCyFZ5e8.

Once students have watched the video give them an opportunity to practice juggling in Modbox. Keep in mind that 20-30 minutes is a recommended time for VR to prevent "eye strain". Please note, It may take more than one 20 minutes session to reach juggling success within Modbox.

Students might want to try juggling with scarves once they have finished with the Modbox experience. Once they have mastered juggling with scarves, they might try juggling with real balls in the physical world.

Post-Application Guidelines & Reflections

Once the student/user has explored and navigated through the VR experience they should answer the following questions:

- Was the use of VR and Modbox effective in helping you juggle quickly?
- What are some drawbacks to using VR and Modbox for scaffolding the learning experience?
- Give an example of another skill or process that might be scaffolded in VR using Modbox to make mastery of learning quicker and easier.

Extension Activities

- The terms "Natural", "Gifted" and "Prodigy" refer to people who have skills or talents that are exceptional at a young age. Research someone in society who you think fits this category and write a report about them.
- Design a scaffolded experience in Modbox to learn how to do archery, bowling or some other sport/hobby by control factors that make the experience easier to master inside Modbox.

Lesson Guide: VR and Eco-tourism
The Blue VR

Designed by Craig Frehlich B.Ed., M.Ed.

© 2019 Springboard Virtual Reality, Inc.

Target Age:	Target Subject/Field:	Essential Idea:
10-adult, Grade 5 and up	Science, Geography/Conservation	Can VR enhance our relationship with nature and promote virtual eco-tourism?

Goal of the Learning Application:
Can immersive VR help us build relationships with nature? Thousands of people around the world spend money to view wildlife in their natural habitat. Is this a sustainable practice? Are eco-tours doing more harm than good? Take a whale-watching, for example. With the boat gas and danger of having a negative encounter, are we helping the whales? Could there be a more environmentally friendly alternative? What about immersive VR? The Blu offers users a close-up encounter with whales and other ocean life. Experience the wonder and majesty of the ocean through a series of habitats and come face to face with some of the most awe-inspiring species on the planet. Is this the new eco-tourism?

Possible Learning Objectives:	Key Concepts & Vocabulary:
<ul><li>Students will be able to develop a greater appreciation for protecting nature.</li><li>Students will be able to understand the impact human activity has on ecosystems.</li><li>Students will reflect on how technology might promote sustainability and conservation.</li><li>Students will evaluate how technology might enhance our relationship with nature.</li></ul>	<ul><li>Sustainability</li><li>Animal Welfare</li><li>Systems</li><li>Conservation</li><li>Relationships</li><li>Eco-tourism</li></ul>

Pre-Application Guidelines & Questions:

Before entering the VR application, users should answer the following questions.
- What is eco-tourism?
- How does it increase sustainability?
- What are the dangers of eco-tourism?
- Have a look at this video, https://www.youtube.com/watch?v=XepmLtD_ads. What are the benefits of watching whales in the wild?

Appendix G 141

- What are the dangers or drawbacks of observing whales in their natural habitat?
- Have a look at this video, https://www.youtube.com/watch?v=Y5R4PZMxDxo&feature=emb_logo. What tips are suggested for watching whales in an ethical manner?
- Watch this video, https://www.youtube.com/watch?v=zJCD3R3LlSs. Do you think that VR can be used for conservation? Why or why not?

Important Tips & Tricks to Consider Inside this VR Application

What to expect? This VR experience should last approximately 10 minutes.
This application has three experiences: The Whale Encounter, The Reef Migration and Luminous Abyss. It is recommended that users try Whale Encounter and then The Reef Migration. **The Luminous Abyss might be a bit scary for first-time users to VR.**

Post-Application Guidelines & Reflections

Once the student/user has explored and navigated through the VR experience, they should answer the following questions:

- What was your favourite part of this experience? What was the most surprising part?
- From the two experiences, Whale Encounter and Reef Migration, which one did you enjoy more and why?
- Do you think the Whale encounter could be a good substitute for real-life whale watching? Explain.
- Have a look at this video, https://www.youtube.com/watch?v=6F4Pfgo730Q. Do you think we should ban people from visiting The Great Barrier Reef and promote VR applications like The Reef Migration?
- Do you think this VR experience may be considered as virtual eco-tourism? Why or why not?
- Although this VR experience is realistic, what are some of its limitations?
- How could this VR experience be improved?

Extension Activities

- Have users engage in the various lessons developed by National Geographic on marine conservation located here, https://www.nationalgeographic.org/unit/marine-ecology-human-impacts-conservation/.
- Watch this award-winning documentary called "Chasing Coral," https://www.chasingcoral.com/.

Appendix G

Lesson Guide: Conflict Resolution Tactics
Smashbox Arena

Designed by Craig Frehlich B.Ed., M.Ed.

© 2019 Springboard Virtual Reality, Inc.

Target Age: 12-Adult, Grade 7 and up	Target Subject/Field: Social studies, History/Conflict Tactics	Essential Idea: Establishing a position of power may be beneficial to resolve conflict.

Goal of the Learning Application:
How do we deal with conflict? Sometimes establishing a position of power in a dispute can provide a distinct advantage. High ground is an area of elevated terrain, which can be useful in competitions that involve combat or conflict. Fighting from an elevated position is supposedly more advantageous as this position gives a person a wider field of view for surveillance. Having the high ground may provide a strategic area of power. Students will be involved in a friendly game of conflict to evaluate whether having high ground offers a distinct advantage in battle. Smashbox Arena is a VR dodgeball game of the future. The user teams up against bots in a fast-paced strategy game whereby tactics can provide an edge in the game.

Possible Learning Objectives:	Key Concepts & Vocabulary:
<ul><li>Students will be able to analyse strategies to establish positions of power in conflicts.</li><li>Students will be able to make inferences and draw conclusions related to geographic positions in conflict and combat.</li><li>Students will be able to demonstrate leadership by initiating and employing various strategies to resolve conflicts.</li><li>Students will be able to use technology to solve a problem or gain a new perspective on an issue.</li></ul>	<ul><li>Power</li><li>Authority</li><li>Perspective</li><li>Strategy</li><li>Conflict Resolution</li></ul>

Pre-Application Guidelines & Questions:
Before users enter the VR applications have them reflect by answering the following questions;
- What does the saying "king of the castle" mean?
- How does having a strategic position of high ground benefit in combat situations like dodgeball? Explain.

- What are some disadvantages to being in a position of high ground?
- Research a historical event whereby having the position of high ground was not advantageous.

Important Tips & Tricks to Consider Inside this VR Application

What to expect?

When the user enters the application, they are presented with several options. One is the tutorial or training option. Pick this first. The user is given training instructions on how to move or teleport, how to pick up, block and shoot balls, how to use particular tools like grenade balls, heatseeker balls, and sniper balls. The tutorial will take approximately 14 minutes.

Once the tutorial is over, you will be taken back to the central building. Next, the user should teleport to the rocket ship that says "story mode." Then, the user will be asked to pick a difficulty level. The user should pick "easy." The game will begin shortly. The strategy for the user or player should be to always play on top of high objects. This is the high ground strategy. So, anytime in the game teleport to achieve this high ground status. Allow the user to play for approximately 15 minutes.

Post-Application Guidelines & Reflections

Once the student/user has explored and navigated through the VR experience, they should answer the following questions:

- Was it advantageous to have the high ground while playing Smashbox? Explain.
- What other factors affected your success in the game? Explain.
- Read this article about modern-day air traffic control towers, https://www.straitstimes.com/singapore/airport-with-no-air-traffic-control-tower. Do you think monitoring airplanes is more effective with this type of air traffic control?
- What is the moral meaning of the saying "take the high ground"? How is it related to having a position of high ground in combat?
- Besides having the high ground, what are some other strategies that could be employed to gain a strategic advantage for the game Smashbox?
- In modern-day conflict or war, is having the high ground still a good strategy during disputes?
- Height can be a distinct advantage. In life, do you think being tall is more advantageous than being short? Explain
- In this learning activity, you were asked to critic whether having a position of power was beneficial in resolving a conflict. Give an example of when it is more advantages to establish a position of power to resolve a conflict.

Extension Activities
- Watch the 1982 movie, Gandhi. You can see the trailer here, https://www.youtube.com/watch?v=B7I6D3mSYTE. Write a report on how Gandhi dealt with conflict resolution.
- Medieval castles were designed with the idea that having the high ground provided a position of power. Research these types of castles and re-design one in a free architectural program like Sketchup, which can be found here, https://www.sketchup.com/plans-and-pricing/sketchup-free.

Bibliography

"About Us—Virtual Reality Institute of Health and Exercise." n.d. https://vrhealth.institute/about/.
Abstract (Season 2)—Ruth Carter: Costume Designer. Directed by Netflix. 2019. Netflix, 2019.
"Acron: Attack of the Squirrels!" SpringboardVR. Accessed January 26, 2020. https://springboardvr.com/marketplace/acronattackofthesquirrels.
AltspaceVR. AltspaceVR Inc. Last modified December 29, 2014. https://altvr.com/.
Anonymous Grade 10 Student. Personal Interview. Singapore. October 5, 2019.
Anonymous Grade 12 Student. Personal Interview. Singapore. December 13, 2019.
"Asymmetric Multiplayer." TV Tropes. n.d. https://tvtropes.org/pmwiki/pmwiki.php/Main/AsymmetricMultiplayer.
"Audioshield." SpringboardVR. Accessed January 26, 2020. https://springboardvr.com/marketplace/audioshield.
Bailenson, Jeremy. *Experience on Demand: What Virtual Reality Is, How It Works, and What It Can Do.* New York: W. W. Norton & Company, 2018.
"Becoming Homeless: A Human Experience." VHIL. Accessed January 26, 2020. https://vhil.stanford.edu/becominghomeless/.
Bernie Dodge, San Diego State University. WebQuest.Org: Home. Accessed January 25, 2020. http://webquest.org.
"Black Hat Cooperative." SpringboardVR. Accessed January 26, 2020. https://springboardvr.com/marketplace/blackhatcooperative.
Brewster, Signe. "Virtual Reality Video Games that Double as Exercise." *The New York Times*—Breaking News, World News & Multimedia. Last modified September 20, 2019. https://www.nytimes.com/2019/09/17/smarter-living/wirecutter/virtual-reality-video-games-that-double-as-exercise.html.
Burger, Edward B., and Michael Starbird. *The 5 Elements of Effective Thinking.* Princeton: Princeton University Press, 2012.
Bye, Kent. "#883 'Rec Room:' Social VR World Building Platform on PC, Console, Mobile, & VR." Voices of VR Podcast. Last modified June 8, 2016. https://voicesofvr.com/883-rec-room-social-vr-world-building-platform-on-pc-console-mobile-vr/.

"Cave Digger." SpringboardVR. Accessed January 26, 2020. https://springboardvr.com/marketplace/cavedigger.

Craig, Emory, and Mia Georgieva. "VR and AR: The Art of Immersive Storytelling and Journalism." EDUCAUSE Review | EDUCAUSE. n.d. https://er.educause.edu/blogs/2018/2/vr-and-ar-the-art-of-immersive-storytelling-and-journalism.

"Crow: The Legend." SpringboardVR. Accessed January 26, 2020. https://springboardvr.com/marketplace/thecrow.

Damiani, Jesse. "The Under Presents? Is a Novel Exploration of VR and Live Immersive Theatre." Forbes. Last modified November 22, 2019. https://www.forbes.com/sites/jessedamiani/2019/11/19/the-under-presents-is-a-novel-exploration-of-vr-and-live-immersive-theatre/#9efa04874556.

David, Anne. "The Push For STEM Education: Why It Matters." TeachThought. Last modified April 16, 2019. https://www.teachthought.com/education/the-push-for-stem-education-why-it-matters/.

Delaney, Melissa. "Survey: Education Among Top Industries for AR/VR Investments." Technology Solutions That Drive Education. Last modified August 8, 2019. https://edtechmagazine.com/k12/article/2019/08/survey-education-among-top-industries-arvr-investments.

ENGAGE Virtual Reality Education & Corporate Training. VR Education Holdings PLC. Last modified August 18, 2015. https://engagevr.io/.

"Equal Reality: Soft Skills, Diversity and Inclusion VR Training." Equal Reality. Last modified August 29, 2018. https://equalreality.com/index.

Erickson, H. L. *Concept-Based Curriculum and Instruction for the Thinking Classroom.* Thousand Oaks: Corwin Press, 2007.

"Escape Room." Wikipedia, the Free Encyclopedia. Last modified March 28, 2013. https://en.wikipedia.org/wiki/Escape_room.

Everything Vive, Zain and Ronnie. Podcast Interview. March 19, 2019.

Fabre, Eve. "Are There Two Pilots in the Cockpit?" The Conversation. Last modified April 11, 2018. http://theconversation.com/are-there-two-pilots-in-the-cockpit-94360.

"Fantastic Contraption." SpringboardVR. Accessed January 26, 2020. https://springboardvr.com/marketplace/fantasticcontraption.

"Fantasy Island." Wikipedia, the Free Encyclopedia. Last modified December 21, 2019. https://en.wikipedia.org/wiki/Fantasy_Island.

Fast Travel Games. "The Curious Tale of the Stolen Pets." Fast Travel Games | Start. Accessed January 26, 2020. https://www.fasttravelgames.com/thecurioustaleofthestolenpets/.

"Firebird—La Peri." SpringboardVR. Accessed January 26, 2020. https://springboardvr.com/marketplace/firebirdlaperi.

"A Fisherman's Tale." SpringboardVR. Accessed January 26, 2020. https://springboardvr.com/marketplace/afishermanstale.

"FORM on Steam." Welcome to Steam. Accessed January 26, 2020. https://store.steampowered.com/app/408520/FORM/.

Gadgeteer | Build Your Dream Machine. Accessed January 26, 2020. https://gadgeteergame.com/.

Gruber, Matthias J., and Charan Ranganath. "How Curiosity Enhances Hippocampus-Dependent Memory: The Prediction, Appraisal, Curiosity, and Exploration (PACE) Framework." *Trends in Cognitive Sciences* 23, no. 12 (2019): 1014–1025.

"Hoops VR." SpringboardVR. Accessed January 26, 2020. https://springboardvr.com/marketplace/hoopsvr.

Inc., VRChat. VRChat. Accessed January 25, 2020. https://www.vrchat.com/.
Johnson, David M., and Roger T. Johnson. "What Is Cooperative Learning?—Cooperative Learning Institute." Cooperative Learning Institute. n.d. http://www.co-operation.org/what-is-cooperative-learning.
Johnson-Glenberg, Mina C. "Immersive VR and Education: Embodied Design Principles that Include Gesture and Hand Controls." *Frontiers in Robotics and AI* 5 (2018).
Kaser, David, Kara Grijalva, and Meredith Thompson. *Envisioning Virtual Reality: A Toolkit for Implementing VR in Education.* Morrisville, NC: Lulu.com, n.d.
Keep Talking and Nobody Explodes. Last modified November 9, 2018. https://keeptalkinggame.com/.
Lanier, Jaron. *Dawn of the New Everything: Encounters with Reality and Virtual Reality.* New York: Henry Holt and Company, 2017.
"Learning, Education & Games, Volume 3—ETC Press." ETC Press. n.d. http://press.etc.cmu.edu/index.php/product/learning-education-games-volume-3/.
"Lesson Planning." Centre for Teaching Excellence. n.d. https://cte.smu.edu.sg/approach-teaching/integrated-design/lesson-planning.
Livio, Mario. *Why?: What Makes Us Curious.* New York: Simon & Schuster, 2017.
"Madeline Hunter Lesson Plan Model." The Second Principle. Last modified May 31, 2014. https://thesecondprinciple.com/essential-teaching-skills/models-of-teaching/madeline-hunter-lesson-plan-model/.
"Manifest 99." SpringboardVR. Accessed January 26, 2020. https://springboardvr.com/marketplace/manifest99.
Mannion, James. *Growth Headset: Exploring the Use of Virtual Reality and Augmented Reality in Schools.* Rethinking Education, 2018. https://iscdigital.co.uk/wp-content/uploads/2018/11/Growth-headset-final-reportV2.pdf.
Marx, Patricia. "Taking Virtual Reality for a Test Drive." *The New Yorker.* Last modified December 2, 2019. https://www.newyorker.com/magazine/2019/12/09/taking-virtual-reality-for-a-test-drive?utm_campaign=VR%20News&utm_content=107451298&utm_medium=social&utm_source=twitter&hss_channel=tw-1120244738.
"MasterpieceVR." SpringboardVR. Accessed January 26, 2020. https://springboardvr.com/marketplace/masterpiecevr.
Matney, Lucas. "Vrse CEO Chris Milk Talks VR Storytelling and the Road to Virtual Reality's Citizen Kane—TechCrunch." TechCrunch. Last modified May 10, 2016. https://techcrunch.com/2016/05/10/vrse-ceo-chris-milk-talks-vr-storytelling-and-the-road-to-virtual-realitys-citizen-kane/.
Milk, Chris. "How Virtual Reality Can Create the Ultimate Empathy Machine." TED: Ideas Worth Spreading. Last modified March 7, 2015. https://www.ted.com/talks/chris_milk_how_virtual_reality_can_create_the_ultimate_empathy_machine.
Miller, Jake. "Marcia Kish, Blended Learning, Seesaw, Student Ownership, Learning Environments, Classroom Balance, Adjacent Possible, Focusing on Verbs More Than Nouns." Free Podcast Hosting—Starting a Podcast in 5 Minutes | Podbean. Last modified January 22, 2020. https://www.podbean.com/media/share/dir-4f6w8-6d34c88?utm_campaign=w_share_ep&utm_medium=dlink&utm_source=w_share.
Mlodinow, Leonard. *Elastic: Flexible Thinking in a Constantly Changing World.* London: Penguin UK, 2018.
"MYP Arts Subject Brief." International Education—International Baccalaureate®. n.d. https://www.ibo.org/globalassets/digital-toolkit/brochures/myp-brief_arts_2015.pdf.

"MYP Individuals and Society Subject Brief." International Education—International Baccalaureate®. n.d. https://www.ibo.org/globalassets/digital-toolkit/brochures/myp-brief_individuals-societies_2015.pdf.

"MYP Language and Literature Subject Brief." IBO. Accessed January 26, 2020. https://www.ibo.org/globalassets/digital-toolkit/brochures/myp-brief_language-literature_2015.pdf.

"MYP Physical Education and Health Subject Brief." International Education—International Baccalaureate®. n.d. https://www.ibo.org/globalassets/digital-toolkit/brochures/myp-brief_phys-health-ed_2015.pdf.

"MYP Science Subject Brief." International Education—International Baccalaureate®. n.d. https://www.ibo.org/globalassets/digital-toolkit/brochures/myp-brief_sciences_-2015.pdf.

"New Research Shows Declining Interest in STEM." Government Technology State & Local Articles—E.Republic. Last modified June 11, 2018. https://www.govtech.com/education/k-12/New-Research-Shows-Declining-Interest-in-STEM.html.

Paller, Ken A., and Joel L. Voss. "Accurate Recognition Based on Explicit versus Implicit Memory." *PsycEXTRA Dataset* (2008).

Peterson, Kay, and David A. Kolb. *How You Learn Is How You Live: Using Nine Ways of Learning to Transform Your Life*. Oakland, CA: Berrett-Koehler Publishers, 2017.

"Project Oxygen—Google Spent 10 Years Researching What Makes the Perfect Manager." Eden Tech Labs. Last modified December 10, 2019. https://www.edentechlabs.io/post/project-oxygen-google-spent-10-years-researching-what-makes-the-perfect-manager.

"Rec Room on Steam." Welcome to Steam. Accessed January 25, 2020. https://store.steampowered.com/app/471710/Rec_Room/.

RoboCo Dev Blog. Last modified March 29, 2019. https://roboco.co/.

Rousell, Michael. Michael Rousell—The Power of Surprise. Last modified November 30, 2018. http://michaelrousell.com/.

Sanders, James, and Mark Hammons. Breakout EDU. n.d. https://www.breakoutedu.com/.

Schrier, Karen. *Learning, Education & Games, Volume 3: 100 Games to Use in the Classroom & Beyond*. Morrisville, NC: Lulu.com, n.d.

"SculptrVR." SpringboardVR. Accessed January 26, 2020. https://springboardvr.com/marketplace/sculptrvr.

Shultz, Ryan. Podcast Interview. Accessed December 13, 2019. https://cfrehlich.podbean.com/e/episode-23-social-vr-and-education-with-ryan-schultz/.

Spencer, John. "What Two Cooking Shows Taught Me about Design Thinking." John Spencer. Last modified March 29, 2019. http://www.spencerauthor.com/what-two-cooking-shows-taught-me-about/.

Stone, Zara. "Why Teachers Are Asking Students to Escape from the Classroom." The Atlantic. Last modified July 28, 2016. https://www.theatlantic.com/education/archive/2016/07/the-rise-of-educational-escape-rooms/493316/.

"The Story of Amanda Todd and the Horrific Effects of Cyberbullying." UBC Blogs. Last modified November 7, 2018. https://blogs.ubc.ca/course0512e7b9763eca9657ab083805266162ded14194/2018/11/07/the-story-of-amanda-todd-and-the-horrific-effects-of-cyberbullying/.

Summers, Rosie. Podcast Interview. https://cfrehlich.podbean.com/e/episode-24-vr-and-art-with-rosie-summers/December 16, 2019.

"TheBlu: Season 1 (Home Edition)." SpringboardVR. Accessed January 26, 2020. https://springboardvr.com/marketplace/thebluhome.

Thompson, Meredith, Anne Wang, Dan Roy, and Eric Klopfer. "Authenticity, Interactivity, and Collaboration in VR Learning Games." Frontiers. n.d. https://www.frontiersin.org/articles/10.3389/frobt.2018.00133/full#B1.

"Tilt Brush on Steam." Welcome to Steam. Accessed January 26, 2020. https://store.steampowered.com/app/327140/Tilt_Brush/.

Trilling, Bernie, and Charles Fadel. *21st Century Skills: Learning for Life in Our Times*. Hoboken, NJ: John Wiley & Sons, 2012.

UN Virtual Reality—United Nations Virtual Reality (UNVR), a Project Implemented by the UN SDG Action Campaign. n.d. http://unvr.sdgactioncampaign.org/.

Valve. "Steam Search." Welcome to Steam. Accessed January 26, 2020. https://store.steampowered.com/search/?term=puzzle.

"Virtual Reality 101: What You Need to Know about Kids and VR." Common Sense Media: Age-Based Media Reviews for Families. n.d. https://www.commonsensemedia.org/research/virtual-reality-101.

"Where Thoughts Go." SpringboardVR. Accessed January 26, 2020. https://springboardvr.com/marketplace/wherethoughtsgo.

About the Author

Craig Frehlich has been working in education for over 25 years and has his master's degree in education with a focus on curriculum design. He is also an educational consultant and speaker on the topics of inquiry, design thinking, and the use of technology in education. His main focus is to use contextual and conceptual thinking to translate VR experiences into lesson guides that help map successfully introspective journeys in virtual reality.

www.ingramcontent.com/pod-product-compliance
Lightning Source LLC
Chambersburg PA
CBHW030140240426
43672CB00005B/199